The Finders

A play by Alan Dapré

Activities by
**Esmonde Banks
and Laura Russell**

2633

PEARSON

Heinemann is an imprint of Pearson Education Limited, Edinburgh Gate,
Harlow, Essex, CM20 2JE.

www.heinemann.co.uk

Heinemann is a registered trademark of Pearson Education Limited.

Play text © Alan Dapré 2012
Activities text © Pearson Education 2012
Typeset by Phoenix Photosetting, Chatham, Kent, UK
Cover design by Kerry Leslie

The right of Alan Dapré to be identified as author of this work has been asserted by
him in accordance with the Copyright, Designs and Patents Act 1988.

First published 2012

16 15 14 13 12
11 10 9 8 7 6 5 4 3 2 1

British Library Cataloguing in Publication Data
A catalogue record for this book is available from the British Library.

ISBN 9780435075439

Printed in China (CTPS/01)

Contents

Teaching resources

To help deliver the questions and activities on pages 86–98, teaching materials are available to download free from www.heinemann.co.uk/literature

Introduction

By Alan Dapré

Writing a play like *The Finders* was an exciting challenge. I have toyed with the notion of an alien abduction story for a while but would only write one if it delivered a satisfying twist. Obviously an introduction is not the best place to tell you about the end of a play in case I give too much away. What I can share is the thought that got me started: having your friends whisked off and knowing you're next.

When I write, I like my characters to interact with the narrative and each other in dramatic and unexpected ways. The story needs to take the reader along for the ride, so slowly plodding about is not an option. It helps if characters have a believable back story – a history that attracts, repels or propels them. While reading or performing, you will discover the characters' hopes, fears and secrets. Even the adult characters are not immune, and they must have their own emotional spark.

The ten character parts use a broad range of vocabulary and speaking styles so that each is real and distinguishable from the others. Therefore, while Tank is blunt and direct, Kiran is more verbally eloquent. Both, however, hide inner frustrations and feel they don't belong. Belonging is the key theme in this play, mirrored by not belonging.

- Jack makes jokes because he feels uncomfortable with Kiran's cleverness, despite their being firm friends.
- Lacking confidence, Nina uses fashion to make herself stand out in the group. Seen as shallow, Nina actually appreciates the value of true friendship.
- Isla feels she and Kiran belong together, despite the fact he can be so distant.
- Kiran's parents share a strong bond with their son but fear it may never last.

- Professor Anderson is happy to belong on the archaeological site doing what she loves most, while Mr Grant seeks freedom from the classroom after teaching inside for so long.
- What of the Finders? Time will tell what they seek and where they belong in the narrative.

The Finders is a play written to be read or performed by Key Stage 3 students. A sense of place can easily be achieved with a few strategic props and some imagination. (More information on staging can be found in the 'Staging suggestions' section on pages vii–xii.) The settings range from inside a school to the middle of Wulder Woods. Slowly the certainties of the characters are stripped away and an uneasy fear builds. People begin to doubt themselves and each other, leading to tension and disputes, anger and despair. Everyone is drawn to the clearing and a realisation that we are all never quite what we seem.

Throughout the story we also get flashes of humour and amazing displays of courage and resilience, friendship and trust. Let us not forget hope. This play is full of the healing power of hope. And hope gives my characters something to hold on to, something that binds them together . . . something that makes them human. Us human.

As for me, my hope is you enjoy reading *The Finders* as much as I enjoyed writing it.

Cast list

The pupils

Jack   *Loves attention but is well liked and fair. He likes to have the last word and has a great sense of humour.*

Tank   *Sporty and muscled. He lacks confidence in his abilities off the sports field and is secretly jealous of Kiran's cleverness.*

Isla   *Sensible and well respected by pupils and staff for her straight-talking honesty. She is Kiran's first girlfriend and is attracted by his quirky mind.*

Kiran   *Quiet and unadventurous and always the outsider in the group. He is hardworking, intelligent and interested in astronomy.*

Nina   *Sparky and fun to be with. Thinks Kiran is dull and needs livening up. She adores fashion and is never without some designer gear.*

Other characters

Mr Grant *A teacher. He is strict but fair and expects pupils to do what he says when he says it. He has high hopes for Kiran.*

Professor Anderson *An archaeologist. She is trendy and cool. She is keen for pupils to enjoy learning about archaeology, which is her passion.*

The Finder *An alien being. The Finder is an unseen presence whose voice is heard communicating its wishes.*

Mum   *Kiran's mother. Warm and protective.*

Dad   *Kiran's father. Deeply loving, strong and comforting. Proud of his relationship with Kiran.*

Note: If necessary, *Mum* and *Dad* can be played by those playing *Professor Anderson* and *Tank*, and the words of *The Finder* can be said alternately by those playing *Jack*, *Isla* and *Nina*.

Staging suggestions

The way that any director or any cast approaches staging a play is bound to be only one way of looking at the text. Even the oldest plays are endlessly reinterpreted as we continue to find new ways of looking at them. Quite simply, there is no right or wrong way to stage a piece, but there are ways which offer greater or lesser challenges to actors and audiences. These staging suggestions will depend more on developing a strong ensemble feel within your cast than they will on bulky and costly sets. As a theatre-goer, I feel the drama starts to die the moment a curtain closes and you hear the scenery trundling around, and it can take a long time to regain lost momentum. I always want the story and the characters to keep moving. I think audiences are happy to suspend disbelief and use their own imaginations if you reward them with a performance that has wit, charm, style and vision, even if you are working in a limited or limiting space.

The Finders is not a ponderous tale. It is a densely packed adventure and I think it should be performed as such. The young characters are playful and robust, with moments of tenderness. If the piece is approached urgently, then any slower moments will stand out as poignant and touching instead of slow.

The locations that need to be defined in *The Finders* are as follows:

- a school
- a street
- Wulder Woods
- the chalet
- an alien spacecraft.

These need to be created with minimum fuss to help the story along. Some settings we spend a decent amount of time in and return to; some last just a few minutes. Try not to waste energy and resources on a setting which is only a page or two long.

I would suggest the following:

Costumes

Much of the staging suggestions below are drawn with a light touch, so audiences may need other (simpler) clues about spaces and characters. For this reason I suggest keeping the costume fairly naturalistic. School shirts and ties, bags, suits and Wellington boots will all help an audience know where they are in the tale. Costumes can be changed, added to or covered up with much less fuss than moving sets around.

Light

Light is a key element in the play; it is a force to be reckoned with, not just a way of seeing what is going on. Use this creatively across the whole performance, making an asset of its possibilities. Consider starting the *event* before the play begins; as the audience enter they could be presented with a gloomy darkness broken by occasional pinpoints of light coming from all angles – these need not be stage lights; torches will do just as well. Perhaps some atmospheric music which hints at an extraterrestrial element might help too.

Staging blocks

Consider using multi-purpose blocks of differing sizes as a main part of your set. If the faces on the boxes are painted differently (for instance; plain wood, white, earth-tones, silvered), they can help to add colour and texture to scenes throughout the play.

Flats

I would suggest creating your set using perhaps half a dozen double-sided free-standing flats (around the size of a large door and preferably on wheels). The flats will help delineate the space, giving opportunities to enter and exit from and hide behind.

These can be constructed simply from timber and canvas and offer all sorts of possibilities. One side of these flats should be painted, fairly impressionistically, with the greens and browns of the trees. The other side should be painted cream/white.

Transitions

Gaps between scenes should be kept to an absolute minimum. I am always happy if performers start to act even as the scene comes together around them, but there still may be moments where the audience feels 'nothing is happening'. Fill these dead spaces with low light and sound effects to create an ominous atmosphere. It would be great if the audience felt that there was something watching, waiting.

Don't forget that an audience's experience doesn't end with the last words of the play. As the cast applaud and as the public exit, consider using music themed with the piece (as in *ET*, *Close Encounters*, etc). It will make them feel more like they have been immersed in your world for a while.

Scenes

School (Scene 1.1)
Bright but unnatural light hits the stage. Sound effect of a school bell and the kind of vocal commotion all schools have in the corridors. As this happens the characters (not scene-shifters or stage managers) run on with their own desks and chairs, ideally using the blocks here (instead of real desks/chairs), which can be sat on, stood on, hidden behind, etc.

A street (Scene 1.2)
A softer, more natural light, the sound of cars, horns, voices, etc. Staging blocks can form a wall or a bench to give the actors some scenery. Other actors (with a coat or jacket on) can walk past to give a sense of 'bustle'. My instinct is to not have Kiran and Isla walking through this scene, but giving them some 'business' to

do (fiddling with a suitcase lock, tying shoelaces, buttoning coats, etc.) before they hurry off.

A clearing in Wulder Woods (Scenes 1.3, 2.1, 2.2, 2.4, 3.1, 3.2, 3.4)

This is the space where much of the real action takes place. It forms the heart of the piece. Sound of birds. Dappled light. Consider using coloured gels and gobos to break up large blocks of light.

For this scene and the one deeper in the wood, use the green/brown painted side of the flats. Keep them spread out in the clearing. When the action goes deeper into the woods, bring the flats closer to give a feeling of claustrophobia.

An archaeological finds table can be placed in the clearing space, but keep it small and mobile and make sure none of the objects on it move around too easily because the table will come in and out of the action.

In the clearing, use the blocks to create the archaeological trench. Any spare blocks can be used as tree trunks or mounds of earth; they will give actors something to interact with, create different levels and add visual interest.

The chalet accommodation (Scenes 1.4, 1.5, 2.3)

Spin the flats to show the plain white/cream side. Use small hooks or Velcro patches to attach signs – Wulder Woods Activity Centre, Exit, Toilets, Car Park, Broom Cupboard, etc.

The blocks can be configured to create beds with the addition of a few pillows and plain sheets.

The extraterrestrial

There are definitely some staging challenges in *The Finders*. Some can be overcome subtly, but I don't think any full production of this play can 'hint at' or 'suggest' the '*beam of light*'.

The spacecraft (Scenes 3.1, 3.4, Pages 61, 79)

This comes so out of the blue that it needs some attention. A simple yet effective solution might be to use the pale side of the flats as a projection screen and use one or more data projectors to create an extraterrestrial atmosphere. Perhaps slowly swirling, merging streams of pure colour, along with a suitable 'alien' soundtrack, will create this atmosphere. If this feels too abstract, perhaps banks of blinking lights and instrumentations will work as a suitable image.

As the alien ship flies off, we need only see the beam travel on the ceiling of the venue and hear the sound effects of alien engines thundering and roaring to know what has happened. An audience should still be watching the reactions on actors' faces to see what the characters are 'seeing'. If they show us the alien ship leaving with their expressions and gestures, we will see it clearly enough.

Kiran's parents (Scene 3.3, Pages 69–72)

Kiran's parents can emerge from gaps between the flats and directly address the audience, or if technical resources allow, they too could be presented as projections.

The Finder (Scenes 3.1, 3.3, Pages 59–60, 67–9, 73)

We do not see the Finder; we only hear the voice. Consider muting it through a microphone and speaker. Perhaps using the beam of light to represent the Finder will allow Kiran to respond to something other than empty space.

The light beam (Scenes 2.1, 2.2, 3.1, Pages 33–4, 36–42, 61–2)

The beam needs to be striking and have a real sense of threat. If this is the only light present when it '*sweeps up*' or '*swings back*', the actors can use the darkness to easily move offstage or behind a stage flat without being seen. Distraction and diversion will also be useful; getting all the other actors to create sound and movement as a character is 'taken' is a simple but effective way of solving this tricky theatrical challenge.

I hope these suggestions solve, rather than create, challenges. They are intended to give your cast as much responsibility as possible. They aim to give your pupils a sense of the kind of ensemble theatre making which is widely used by companies like Complicité, Kneehigh and Improbable and will develop their performance skills rather than relying on expensive trickery.

Richard Conlon

This play is dedicated to Isla Rose Dapré,
a wee tiger with a big roar.
And Kate, who makes our world rock!

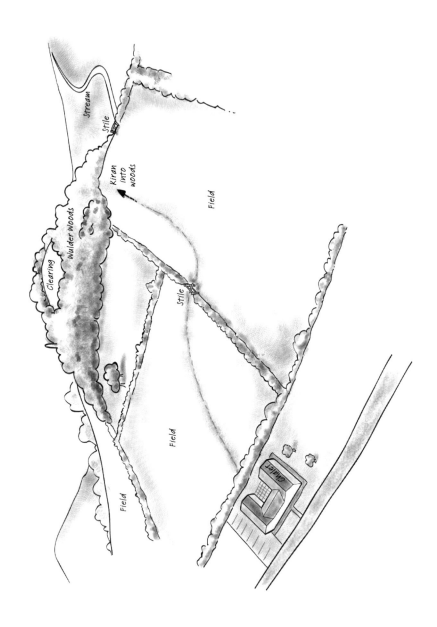

Act One

Scene 1

A classroom during a geography lesson.

There are two rows of desks. Nina and Isla sit in front, alongside Jack. Kiran sits in the second row, with an empty desk between him and Tank. Mr Grant is pacing up and down and gesturing towards a whiteboard. Tank is doodling.

MR GRANT: *(Firmly)* Thomas Arthur Neil Kane! If I wanted this to be an art lesson I would have given you paints.

JACK: *(Stage whisper)* Crayons, more like.

TANK: Yer what? *(He stands, looming)*   5

ISLA: *(Sighs)* Tank by name, Tank by nature.

MR GRANT: Please sit down, Thomas. *(Tank sits, glaring at Jack)* What's that you're drawing?

TANK: Nowt.

Tank crumples the paper he was doodling on into a ball and lobs it into a bin.

JACK: Good shot.   10

TANK: That's why I'm basketball captain and you're not.

JACK: Netball? Did you say netball?

MR GRANT: That's enough, you two. Now, who can summarise in one sentence what we've   15 learned today?

JACK: *(To Isla)* Tank can't draw?

ISLA: *(Not wanting trouble)* Shhh.

MR GRANT: Speak up, Isla.

ISLA: Er . . . siting a settlement is a complex 20
geographical decision because you have to
consider lots of . . . *(brightly)* variables.

MR GRANT: *(Pleased)* Exactly. *(He addresses Jack)* Such as?

JACK: Defending yourself from attacks by
uncivilised people. 25

Jack glances at Tank who scowls.

MR GRANT: Nina?

NINA: Let me think. Hang on.

TANK: She wasn't listening.

NINA: *(Irritated)* I was – actually. Where something
is put depends a lot on key social and 30
economic factors.

MR GRANT: Good.

TANK: *Actually*, she's just repeating what yer said
earlier.

MR GRANT: Then she *really was* listening. Go on, Nina. 35

NINA: *(Brightly)* No one wants to live miles from a
decent shoe shop or a cash machine.

JACK: I'm not sure the Saxons had debit cards, Nina.

NINA: Bet they had credit cards though. Those
gorgeous gold necklace thingies don't 40
come cheap.

MR GRANT: Torcs.

NINA: I'd buy so many torcs I'd rattle.

JACK: She's all torc. *(Laughs)* See what I did there?

MR GRANT:	*(Wearily)* Yes, Jack. In some ways Nina is right. It certainly makes sense to consider available technology when siting a new settlement. 45

Nina looks smug. Mr Grant approaches Kiran who is speed-reading through a geography textbook.

MR GRANT:	So what's your view on technology, Kiran?
JACK:	*(Rolling his eyes)* Here he goes. 50
KIRAN:	*(Shrugging)* We're blasting through space at about eighteen and a half miles per second on a tiny ball of iron with a thin, rocky surface and a feeble layer of water and oxygen. Our star is in a **spiral galaxy** – the Milky Way – travelling along with a couple of hundred billion other stars and we're surrounded by billions of other galaxies . . . 55
NINA:	*(Quietly to Isla)* He lost me at 'We're . . .' 60
ISLA:	*(Whispering back)* You get used to it.
NINA:	Not me. You're both clever. Straight 'A' pupils.
ISLA:	It comes naturally to Kiran. For me it's a slog.
KIRAN:	The Magellanic Clouds are pretty close to us but the nearest galaxy similar to the size of the Milky Way is Andromeda and that is about 2.5 million light-years away. It takes ages to get there. 65
TANK:	*(Tank slumps on his desk, bored)* And ages to explain. 70
NINA:	What's a light-year?

JACK: *(Grins)* Same as a heavy-year but lighter, eh Kiran?

KIRAN: A light-year is the distance light travels in 75 an Earth year, about ten million million kilometres. *(Pauses)* So there are a lot of places to site settlements but we just can't get to them.

JACK: All very impressive, Kiran. But what's that 80 got to do with technology and Saxons?

KIRAN: *(Patiently)* If you have advanced enough technology you can go places. The Angles, Saxons and Jutes came to Britain from Germany, Denmark and southern parts of 85 Sweden and Norway on well-built ships. They settled and in time became Anglo-Saxons. Technology changes. Names change, places change. Everything changes. Nothing lasts forever. Not you. Not me. 90

JACK: Cheery.

The bell rings. Lesson over.

MR GRANT: Not even this lesson.

Tank is first out of his seat. He throws his books into his bag and leaves, passing Kiran.

TANK: Freak. What planet are yer on?

ISLA: *(Puts her arm around Kiran)* Just ignore him.

The other pupils pack up slowly and dawdle to the classroom exit.

JACK: We've been mates since nursery, Kiran, and 95 I still don't understand half of what you say.

Must be weird in that head of yours. All
those complicated facts spinning about and
crashing into each other.

KIRAN: Yeah. *(Smiling)* Like particles colliding in   100
a **linear particle accelerator**.

JACK: Er, if you say so.

NINA: If Kiran's so clever he can tell us this week's
winning lottery numbers. My dad could do
with a new car.   105

ISLA: He's only just bought one!

NINA: Second hand. *(Grumbling)* Rusty. Hardly a
new Mercedes, is it? *(She pauses dreamily)* If I
had a kid I'd call it that.

JACK: Rusty?   110

NINA: Mercedes!

Mr Grant catches up with Kiran.

MR GRANT: You think outside of the box. I like that.

KIRAN: *(Feeling awkward)* Thanks.

MR GRANT: About the field trip next month. I noticed
your name isn't on the list. I'll keep it   115
pinned on the wall for an extra two days.
Just in case.

KIRAN: But you said it was optional.

MR GRANT: True. I can't make pupils come away on a
long weekend.   120

KIRAN: Dad is a bit strapped for cash. Not sure he
can shell out. Says there aren't enough
tourists booking into our holiday cottage.
The takings are already down on last year.

(Smiles) My mum said, on the positive side, 125
she doesn't have to keep changing the beds.

JACK: Was that a joke? *(Clutches his ribs in mock laughter)*

NINA: What's up? You cracked a rib?

JACK: Worse. Kiran cracked a joke.

NINA: Is he feeling okay? 130

MR GRANT: *(Gesturing at Nina and Jack to go)* I'm trying to have a private conversation. *(They drop back)* Now, Kiran, I've already had a word with the headteacher who says there might be a fund we can use. Sounds promising. 135

KIRAN: *(Mumbling)* Sounds like charity.

MR GRANT: *(Sighs)* See it as a gift. A boost for your education. Last parents' evening your mum told me you'd bought a new telescope and spend *every* weekend studying space. I'm 140 sure you could use a break.

KIRAN: I use an **apochromatic refractor telescope**, which gives me sharp, top-quality optical imaging. Astronomy is my life.

MR GRANT: Okay. Wulder Woods is more down to 145 earth but it would be a fascinating experience for you. All that fresh air. No **light pollution**. I'm convinced you'd enjoy it. Have a think and get back to me.

KIRAN: I'll . . . see. 150

Tank appears.

TANK: Nearly forgot. *(Tank hands Mr Grant a crumpled envelope as Jack and Nina catch up)* It's all there –

apart from the two quid I used for snacks. I'll bring that tomorrow.

JACK: Tomorrow's Saturday. 155

TANK: *(Scowling at Jack)* Monday then.

MR GRANT: *(Uneasily)* Thank you, Thomas. Your presence will be most, er, welcome.

With a last scowl at Jack, Tank strides off. Mr Grant follows, unsure what to do with the envelope. He stuffs it into his pocket and coins fall out. Grumbling, he picks them up, dropping his lesson notes. Nina helps pick them up.

JACK: *(To Isla)* You said Tank wasn't coming.

ISLA: I said I hoped he wasn't. *(To Kiran)* But I 160 hope *you* are.

JACK: Useless fact of the day. *(Pause)* Kiran's never been on a school trip.

NINA: Is that true? *(Kiran nods)* Shame you missed the last one. What was it? A trip in the 165 Lakes.

ISLA: Literally for some. *(Pointing at Jack)* Guess who fell head first into the water as he tried to clamber from his canoe?

JACK: Yeah, yeah. Old news. 170

ISLA: Mr Grant was convinced Jack had caught Weil's disease – that disgusting bacterial infection you can get from swallowing rat's urine.

JACK: Well I didn't. I kept my mouth shut. Wish 175 you would.

NINA: *(To Kiran)* Surely your mum will let you come with us this time?

KIRAN: She worries.

ISLA: *(Whispering)* We could have some time   180
together. Just you and me.

JACK: *(Laughing)* That's what she's worried about.

Isla shoots Jack a 'mind your own business' look.

KIRAN: My parents like to know where I am.

NINA: Yeah, cos they don't want their only son lost
forever, deep in some dark woods. Wulder   185
Woods. Woooh! Sounds scary.

JACK: About as scary as Tank's doodle of Mr Grant.

Jack holds up Tank's crumpled doodle.

ISLA: Scarily good. Looks just like him. Particularly
the bolt through the neck. Nice touch.

All the pupils exit.

Blackout.

Scene 2

Outside Kiran's house.

ISLA: Kiran! The minibus is waiting. Mr Grant will
pull his hair out if we're late.

Kiran runs down the path, dragging a huge case.

KIRAN: Won't take him long then.

ISLA: *(Eyeing his case)* We're going to Wulder
Woods not round the world.   5

KIRAN: It's the only case I've got.

ISLA: Don't tell me, you've hidden your telescope in there?

KIRAN: I wish. It wouldn't even fit in this huge thing. Not a bad idea though. The night sky would   10
be perfect above Wulder Woods. No light pollution.

ISLA: *(Happily)* Kiran? I'm glad you're on this field trip.

KIRAN: Mum and Dad were not very thrilled. I'm   15
only going because . . .

ISLA: Because what?

KIRAN: *(Shyly)* Because of you. Us. *Because* we never get time together.

ISLA: We'll sit *together* at the back of the minibus.   20
(Laughs) With Tank. *(Hopefully)* He *might*
leave us alone.

KIRAN: Don't hold your breath.

ISLA: I'll have to when he starts scoffing his family-sized packets of cheese and onion   25
crisps.

KIRAN: Tank reckons he's building up his strength. Jack reckons Tank ran a **half-marathon** last weekend.

ISLA: Probably trying to get away from his four   30
big sisters. It's bad enough having one. I didn't ask to be a twin.

KIRAN: Try being an only child.

ISLA: A whole bedroom to yourself? Bliss.

KIRAN: I've so many gadgets there's hardly any   35

room for me. *(Pause)* I banged on your door yesterday . . . about seven.

ISLA: Sorry, I was over at my gran's.

KIRAN: Which one?

ISLA: The one with the three-legged poodle. 40

KIRAN: Tripod?

ISLA: Trixy!

KIRAN: *(Pause)* I was desperate to get out of the house.

ISLA: Why? 45

They walk along in silence.

KIRAN: Mum was crying all night.

ISLA: That's not like her.

KIRAN: And my dad was staring red-eyed at that **dilapidated** old computer of his. When I came into his office he tried to cover the 50 monitor screen and shut it all down.

ISLA: Sounds suspicious.

KIRAN: Yeah. I glimpsed numbers counting down in the corner of the screen. Whirring dead fast. *(Pause)* And the rest of the screen had a 55 simple star map. Of space. Deep space.

ISLA: Maybe he's getting into astronomy like you?

KIRAN: Dad's a typical newbie. Obsessed. He uses my telescope more than I do. Every night this month he's been in my room. Staring 60 into space . . . hours, like . . . until I have to tell him to go to bed so I can go to sleep.

ISLA: And there's your mum thinking it's you who's always staring at the stars.

KIRAN: I don't like to tell her it's Dad. I know you 65 think *I'm* odd but he's been acting *really* strange recently.

ISLA: What sort of strange?

KIRAN: Soppy strange. Producing embarrassing old photos of me. Ruffling my hair like he used 70 to when I was a kid. Not like him at all.

ISLA: No big deal really. It's only a long weekend. You'll be home in no time.

KIRAN: *(Brightly)* Yeah.

They exit.

Blackout.

Scene 3

A circular clearing at Wulder Woods (an unexplored archaeological site).

Professor Anderson is standing in a shallow trench, holding a trowel. Kiran, Isla, Jack, Tank and Nina are standing by the trench next to Mr Grant, who is speaking.

MR GRANT: . . . and this is Professor Anderson who is the site supervisor. She is in charge of this dig.

Professor Anderson smiles at Mr Grant, who smiles uncomfortably back.

MR GRANT: Er . . . what she – I mean the professor – says goes. Does everyone understand?

The pupils nod that they understand.

PROFESSOR: I trust your teacher has already gone 5
through the site etiquette with you?

TANK: Ettiwhat?

ISLA: The rules for this place.

TANK: Oh. I knew that.

PROFESSOR: All you need to do is *look* and *think* as you 10
move around the site. Fragile archaeological
layers and **artefacts** are all about you.
Walking over them *will* cause damage. I want
you all to have a great time here, but my first
priority is preserving ancient **relics**. 15

JACK: *(Whispering to Nina)* She means Mr Grant.

MR GRANT: *(Guessing)* No, Jack. She doesn't mean me.

TANK: So **predictable**, Jack.

JACK: Predictable? Oooh – Tank's swallowed a
dictionary. 20

MR GRANT: Any questions for the professor?

ISLA: Could you explain the specific purpose of
this place?

PROFESSOR: *(Enthusiastically)* In a nutshell, no. Our
excavation is at a very early stage. This 25
past month we've put in some test pits and,
as you can see, opened up a trench in this
clearing.

ISLA: But why excavate here? Why not dig in the
field around Wulder Woods? 30

PROFESSOR: Good question. Isla, is it? *(Isla nods)* After
studying **aerial** photographs, old maps and

using GPR – ground penetrating radar – we
chose this site as the most likely to reveal
past occupation. The circular clearing we're   35
standing in is basically a big dip. As yet we
have no hard facts, just interesting theories.
Possibly it's an ancient pool. Or maybe a
midden.

JACK: A what?   40

TANK: A rubbish tip.

PROFESSOR: *(Impressed)* Correct.

JACK: *(Quietly to Tank)* How'd you know that?

TANK: That'd be telling.

JACK: Telly more like.   45

TANK: *(Shrugs)* Documentaries.

PROFESSOR: Any ideas how we would know if it was a
           midden?

NINA: The place would be full of rubbish, like that
           scummy skateboard park on Gateside Street   50
           behind the school.

KIRAN: The waste in a midden sinks down over time
           so you get a dip.

PROFESSOR: *(Pleased with Kiran)* True. Now if this were a
           midden I would expect greater plant   55
           growth above the ground than you see here.
           The soil is unusually bare.

NINA: *(Jumping back)* **Contaminated**?

PROFESSOR: *(Smiling)* Soil samples indicate otherwise. At
           the moment I'm **flummoxed**. The really   60
           odd thing is that we're finding evidence
           of crushing, so . . .

KIRAN: So it could be an impact crater.

TANK: Yeah? *(Excited)* Like a ginormous chunk of space rock smashed into the Earth at a 65 zillion miles an hour and wiped out all the plants and dinosaurs . . . but not cockroaches cos they can survive anything.

NINA: Except school dinners.

PROFESSOR: *(Grins)* An **intriguing hypothesis**. But a 70 **meteor strike** would have heated the ground and altered the make-up of the sandstone rocks. Sandstone contains quartz and if quartz were heated and put under pressure it would become glass, but there 75 is no evidence this has happened. It's all very odd. And very exciting. Which is why it is such a pleasure to share this special site with you pupils this weekend.

MR GRANT: I'm sure everyone is raring to go. 80

Jack nudges Nina.

JACK: Yeah, home. Bored . . . bored . . . bored. Did I say bored?

Nina pretend yawns.

PROFESSOR: *(Holding up a trowel and dustpan)* The tools of the trade. I assume you all know how to handle a dustpan. The trowel takes a little 85 more practice. The trick is to scrape little and often. Like **tickling a trout**.

JACK: *(Whispering)* She's bonkers.

Professor Anderson demonstrates how to scrape debris into the dustpan.

PROFESSOR:	Would anyone like a turn?
NINA:	*(Quietly to Isla)* I have to do that at home. 90 Why would I do it on holiday?
JACK:	You call this a holiday? Give me a paintballing weekend any day.
PROFESSOR:	Kiran?
TANK:	*(Frowning at Kiran)* Knew she'd choose yer. 95

Kiran hesitates by the trench.

MR GRANT:	In you go, Kiran.

Professor Anderson points to a patch of soil and hands the tools to Kiran who scrapes the surface lightly.

PROFESSOR:	Take off a little more soil. *(Kiran does so)* And some more. *(Kiran pauses, unsure)* You can be bolder than that.
JACK:	*(Desperate to do something)* Oh, let me 100 do it!

Jack jumps in the trench, snatches the trowel and digs as if in a sandpit.

PROFESSOR:	No! No! **Cease** and **desist**. It is **imperative** you all respect the archaeology. Please!
MR GRANT:	Jack! *(Jack carries on)* I insist you get out! *(Tank jumps in)* Oh, not you too, Thomas! 105
TANK:	*(Dragging Jack out)* The professor says yer not giving this place respect. Once this old stuff is dug up yer can't put it back.

Letting go of Jack, Tank peers into the trench.

TANK:	Jack, look at what yer clumsy feet have done. *(To Professor Anderson)* Sorry 'bout him. He don't always think.
JACK:	Speak for yourself.
PROFESSOR:	*(Impressed with Tank)* Er, thank you.
TANK:	*(Embarrassed)* No worries.
PROFESSOR:	Mr Grant, I do believe someone requires a quiet word.
MR GRANT:	*(Scowling at Jack)* My pleasure.

Mr Grant passes Jack and beckons him to follow. They talk out of earshot. Mr Grant is clearly unhappy. Everyone looks on except Kiran.

Kiran is staring where Jack has just dug. As he secretly eases out a broken brooch, Isla turns and sees a flash of metal in his hands.

ISLA:	Kiran?
KIRAN:	*(Hiding something)* Yes?
ISLA:	Nothing. You'd better get out before you annoy Tank.
KIRAN:	He's well stoked already.

Tank is striding towards Jack and Mr Grant.

TANK:	Look at him. He don't give a stuff. This ain't a holiday, Jack. We're here to learn from the prof.
JACK:	Maybe she'll teach you some grammar.
TANK:	Maybe I'll teach yer to watch yer mouth.

Mr Grant steps in between the two pupils. He looks at Professor Anderson and sighs.

110

115

120

125

MR GRANT: I'll take them both back to the chalet to cool off.

TANK: It ain't me who's causing grief – it's him. 130
All that digging.

MR GRANT: *(Pause)* Okay. Thomas, you can stay here.
Jack, I want a quiet word. Now!

Mr Grant and Jack start to walk away.

TANK: *(Mocking)* Off to buy a toy bucket and spade?

JACK: *(Jack glares back)* I'll borrow yours. 135

Mr Grant and Jack exit. Professor Anderson kneels in the trench and starts to talk to Nina, Isla and Kiran.

PROFESSOR: What do you know about Wulder Woods? I
gather you undertook some preliminary
studying of maps in class with Mr Grant.

Tank joins the group.

NINA: *(Hushed to Isla)* Did we?

ISLA: We did. You were too busy finishing off 140
your science homework.

PROFESSOR: Nina?

NINA: What do I know? Er, Wulder Woods is
alliteration. Both words begin with the same
letter sound. Sorry, Professor – my English 145
is better than my geography or history.

PROFESSOR: *(Easygoing)* Nice try. Okay, Wulder Woods
was named by the Saxons after an ancient
sky god. Scandinavians knew him as Uller,
'The Brilliant One', and he is linked with 150
the mysterious and beautiful Northern
Lights. Ever heard of them, Nina?

NINA: Ask Kiran. He knows everything.

KIRAN: Not everything. The Northern Lights are known as the *aurora borealis*. 155

NINA: What did I tell you?

KIRAN: *Aurora* means 'a natural lightshow'. Atoms in the upper atmosphere collide with the **solar wind** and are excited so much by the Earth's magnetic field they emit photons of light. 160

PROFESSOR: I'm impressed. *(Pause)* Now, I have collated some maps of the area for you to study.

Professor Anderson goes to search under the finds table.

ISLA: *(Whispering)* That's what I love about you.

KIRAN: *(Bemused)* What?

ISLA: You're such an oddball. 165

KIRAN: Everyone knows about the *aurora borealis*. *Aurora* is a Roman word, *borealis* is Greek.

NINA: It's all geek to me.

Nina and Isla laugh. Kiran joins in.

Blackout.

Scene 4

The chalet accommodation.

Kiran and Jack's room overlooks a field that leads to Wulder Woods. Mr Grant is standing by the door. Kiran and Jack are sitting up in their beds.

MR GRANT: Ten thirty. *(Glancing at his watch)* No . . . ten thirty-one precisely. Which means, boys, it's

| | lights off and sweet dreams. I need you two raring to go tomorrow. The professor will be waiting. | 5 |

KIRAN: Six o'clock start?

MR GRANT: I'm afraid so. There's a lot to get through.

JACK: A lot of cornflakes. Any chance of a bacon roll in the morning?

MR GRANT: That's cooking. Toast and marmalade is about all I can manage. Except I brought apricot jam by mistake. — 10

JACK: Great.

MR GRANT: My two rascals were playing up. Taking things out of the trolley as I was putting them in. — 15

JACK: I'll never have kids.

MR GRANT: Never say never. I said I'd never organise field trips but here we are. Anyway, enough chat. *(Pause)* This reminds me of when I put — 20 my boys to bed. And they're half your age.

JACK: *(In a childish voice)* Will you read us a bedtime story?

MR GRANT: Too late for that.

Mr Grant smiles and switches off the light. The full moon casts a cold glow into the room.

MR GRANT: Night-night. Don't — 25

JACK: Let the bed bugs bite. Yeah, we know.

Mr Grant shuts the door and it clicks loudly.

KIRAN: I don't know anything about bed bugs.

JACK: They bug you in bed. That's all you need to know. Now do as he says and get your head down. 30

KIRAN: Are you going to snore?

JACK: I don't snore.

KIRAN: You did in my two-man tent.

JACK: No way was that a two-man tent. One and a quarter at most. If I did snore it was only 35 cos you had your cheesy foot in my face.

KIRAN: S'pose it was a bit small. Dad was **adamant** I didn't need anything bigger as we were only in the back garden. Hardly base camp on Mount Everest. I got it for my tenth birthday, 40 remember? Instead of a mobile phone with an integrated satellite navigation system.

JACK: Last birthday I told Mum I wanted a sports watch with lap memory, speed and distance tracking and underwater functionality. 45

KIRAN: And?

JACK: And she got me this thing. All it does is tell the time.

KIRAN: I can't sleep.

JACK: I can. You always have to be different. 50

KIRAN: That's why we get on.

JACK: *(Sleepily)* What?

KIRAN: If we were the same it'd be boring.

JACK: Eh?

KIRAN: You get me doing stuff I wouldn't normally 55 do.

JACK: Mountain biking. Jogging. S'pose you do the same for me.

KIRAN: Maths. You would never have understood quadratic equations without me.   60

JACK: *(Jokily)* My life hasn't been the same since. Most of what you say goes right over my head. *(Pause)* I like the fact you just do what you do and don't care what the class thinks. Me, I have to crack jokes all the time.   65

KIRAN: You need their approval.

JACK: *(Pause)* I need to sleep. I'm knackered. My little sis held a sleepover party last night. All I could hear was giggling and seven girls raiding the fridge. *(Grumbling)* Nothing left   70 when I sneaked down at midnight. Just marmalade. I should have brought it with me.

Jack lies back and plumps his pillow noisily. He tosses and turns until he is settled. Kiran stares through the window towards Wulder Woods. Then he simply leans back, bathed in moonlight.

Lights fade down to a blackout then slowly fade up.

Time has clearly passed. Jack is gently snoring.

Kiran pulls a torch from under his pillow. He reaches for his trousers and retrieves the broken half-brooch from his back pocket.

He tries to turn on the torch but it won' t work, even after a shake. Kiran then drops it on his bed and goes to the window. Kiran holds the half-brooch up to the moonlight.

KIRAN: *(Whispering to himself)* Unusual pattern of pinpricks. They let light through. A broken Saxon brooch? Maybe Norse? No, it's stranger than that. Isla would love this. She loves odd things. *(Grins)* Loves me. If I found the other half . . . polished it up . . . it'd be a good birthday present for her.

75

Kiran goes to the window and stares over at Wulder Woods. He begins to walk towards his bed and accidentally kicks a chair. Jack wakes suddenly and sits up.

JACK: *(Sleepily)* What are you doing?

80

KIRAN: I sleepwalk sometimes.

JACK: Get back in bed, eh? You're like an elephant.

KIRAN: Do elephants sleepwalk?

JACK: I haven't asked them.

Kiran sits on his bed. Jack lies back. Kiran secretly studies the half-brooch. Jack lets out a snore. Kiran reaches for his coat, swings it over his shoulders and stands, slipping into his shoes. He glances over at Jack who is facing away.

Kiran picks up the torch and creeps to the door. He silently turns the handle and opens the door, slipping through. He closes the door slowly.

It lets out a loud click. Jack sits up, rubbing his eyes. Jack stares at Kiran's empty bed for a moment then scrabbles out of bed. He grabs his coat and shoes and makes for the door.

Blackout.

Scene 5

A corridor in the chalet outside Jack and Kiran's room. It leads to a kitchen. The corridor is lined with doors marked 'Broom Cupboard', 'Bathroom', 'Car Park Exit'.

Another door opens and Jack appears, cautiously. He closes the door, wincing when it clicks shut.

JACK: *(To the door)* Shhh!

Jack straightens when he hears a clatter from the kitchen. He heads towards the door marked 'Car Park Exit'. The bathroom door opens and Jack dives into the broom cupboard, leaving its door ajar. Mr Grant passes, carrying a toothbrush, pausing only to close the door of the broom cupboard.

Long pause.

Isla and Nina appear from the kitchen. Isla holds a pizza box. Nina is eating a slice, trying not to drip cheese. Jack swings open the broom cupboard door and steps into the corridor – in front of the girls.

Brooms fall out around him – but he catches them all before they make a noise.

ISLA: *(Dropping the pizza box in surprise)* Ahhh!

NINA: *(Choking back her shock – and pizza)* Jack! That's not funny.

JACK: Shhh! 5

NINA: Don't shush me. *(Grumbling)* You've ruined our pizza.

Jack puts the brooms back.

JACK: *(Whispering)* Where did you get that beauty from?

ISLA: The kitchen. 10

JACK: Give me some.

ISLA: *(Points down)* You're welcome.

Jack picks a slice up off the floor. Takes a bite.

NINA: That's disgusting.

JACK: Yeah. Why put pepperoni with tuna?

ISLA: I happen to prefer it. Well, not now. 15

Isla scoops the pizza back into the box, which is left on the floor. Jack jokily offers her his slice.

JACK: More for me.

NINA: Enjoy . . . *(Still disgusted)* The cooker's still warm. There's another pizza in the kitchen freezer you could have.

JACK: And how did it get there? 20

NINA: I sneaked them in while Mr Grant was unpacking.

JACK: Look, ladies, I'd like to stay and share a lovely moment – and pizza – with you but I'm kinda busy. 25

ISLA: *(Suddenly worried)* Where's Kiran?

JACK: Who knows? My guess is he's somewhere outside.

NINA: Wulder Woods?

JACK: *(Nodding)* That's what I reckon. 30

NINA: What's he doing outside? It's bad enough us sneaking around inside . . . but outside? Mr Grant will go ballistic if he finds out.

JACK: He won't find out. I'm gonna bring Kiran back before he gets into trouble. My mate would do that for me.   35

NINA: Would he?

JACK: *(Pause)* Maybe not.

ISLA: Are you sure Kiran is out there? *(To Nina)* Perhaps he's still in the chalet looking for   40
me . . . us?

NINA: *(Unconvinced)* Perhaps.

JACK: Don't think so.

Jack runs down the corridor and looks out of a side window.

ISLA: Can you see him?

JACK: There's a shadowy figure at the top of the   45
field. Either a zombie scarecrow or your BF.

ISLA: He's not my boyfriend.

NINA: That's not what you said in the kitchen.

ISLA: *(Hissing)* You don't have to broadcast it.

JACK: *(Grinning)* Everyone knows. Even Mr Grant.   50

ISLA: Oh, Jack. You didn't tell *him*?

JACK: Didn't need to. The fact you sat next to your BF every morning during form time was enough of a clue.

NINA: I sat next to you last week.   55

JACK: That was detention. Different thing. Unless

you secretly have a crush on me. If you do I'd understand.

NINA: *If* I did I'd seek medical treatment.

Isla stands by the window staring at Wulder Woods.

NINA: What now?   60

JACK: I'm going after him. Kiran might be crazy enough to date Isla but he's still my best mate.

NINA: Crazy enough to go wandering in the woods at midnight?

JACK: *(Shrugs)* Reckon so. You coming?   65

NINA: *(Points to her night clothes)* Dressed like this? Wait.

Nina runs off. Jack and Isla both look out of the window. Nina returns with two coats.

ISLA: *(Isla hesitates as she takes her coat)* Thank you.

JACK: You seem nervous.

ISLA: Should we be doing this?   70

NINA: He's your boyfriend. *You* should definitely do something.

JACK: Unless you'd rather go running to Mr Grant?

ISLA: We could say Kiran is sleepwalking.

JACK: In your dreams. The less Baldilocks-and-   75
the-three-hairs knows the better. Let's go.

Jack opens the door to the car park. He steps outside. Isla follows. Nina zips up her coat, shivers and follows her friends.

Blackout.

Act Two

Scene 1

Wulder Woods.

Jack, Nina and Isla stand at the edge of the tree line while bats screech above.

NINA: *(Wiping her boots on grass)* My suede boots are trashed.

ISLA: Nina, the sludge will brush off.

NINA: Ew – my dad hates cleaning them.

JACK: Wouldn't harm if you did it.   5

NINA: As if. *(Waves her fingers in front of Jack)* New nails . . . perfectly polished.

JACK: *(Sarcastically)* Just like the rest of you, eh?

NINA: I'm ultra cultured. Looking this good is an art form.   10

JACK: It's just finger painting.

Nina gives him a half-playful push.

NINA: Where now?

JACK: We go into the trees.

NINA: You're joking. Can't we just wait for Kiran to come out?   15

JACK: We can't just wait. Mr Grant might see us hanging about the top of this field.

ISLA: *(Seriously)* Kiran will be in the clearing – I know it.

JACK: Digging up trouble.   20

NINA: What is he thinking?

JACK: Who knows?

ISLA: *I* never know. It's easier to stand back and let Kiran drift along in his own weird world.

JACK: So . . . you wanna give up? Is that what you girls are saying?   25

ISLA: No. I want to do this.

> *Isla disappears into the shadowy undergrowth ahead.*

NINA: *(Nudging Jack)* Don't let Isla go in there by herself.

JACK: *(Irritated) We* won't. Come on. Your razor-sharp nails will scare anything off.   30

NINA: Shame about your razor-sharp wit. *(Nina hurries onward then stops, peering down)* Ew. My boots are leaking!

JACK: *(Teasing)* Fashion victim.   35

> *Jack helps Nina out of a patch of wet mud and into Wulder Woods.*

> *Blackout.*

> *Lights up, dimmer than before.*

ISLA: The clearing can't be far now.

NINA: Good, because I am totally grossed out by Nature. Did you see those bats? They dived right at me.

JACK: It's your long hair. *(Chuckling)* Bats roost upside down in designer hair extensions.   40

NINA: *(Rolling her eyes)* Yeah, right.

A bat screeches suddenly, frighteningly loud. Nina screams and crouches, clutching her hair.

ISLA: It's gone, Nina.

NINA: *(Sobbing)* Can't we just go? I mean, Kiran's probably back at the chalet by now.   45

JACK: Go if you like. I'm not leaving till I check out this clearing.

ISLA: *(Strongly)* Me neither.

NINA: *(Standing up and grumbling)* Oh, let's get it over with then.   50

Nina pushes past Isla and Jack and stomps into the clearing.

ISLA: Look out for the trench.

NINA: I'm not daft. *(Nina falls in)* Arrgghh!

Isla runs up with Jack.

NINA: It's okay. I'm okay. *(Stumbling to her feet)*

JACK: *(Shrugs)* She's okay.

NINA: But I don't know about him.   55

Isla, Jack and Nina peer further along the trench. Kiran is crouched on the clay, gouging wildly with his torch and fingertips.

ISLA: *(Gasping)* Kiran!

Jack jumps into the trench and takes hold of Kiran's shoulders. Jack easily gets shrugged off and tumbles back into Nina.

Both fall to the ground.

NINA: *(Upset)* My white denim jacket with button-through front fastening is filthy.

JACK: *(To Nina)* Sorry?

NINA: It's a girl thing.   60

JACK: What's up with Kiran?

Isla approaches slowly. Kiran is wildly gouging the clay, oblivious to her presence.

Isla kneels and tenderly hugs Kiran. He swings his head round and stares at her, wide-eyed and as though in a trance.

ISLA: Kiran. It's me. Isla.

Kiran turns away and digs once more. A helpless Isla looks over at her friends.

NINA: *(To Jack)* Do something.

JACK: You do something!

NINA: *(Pushing Jack forward)* You get one arm.   65
        We'll get the other.

Jack runs at Kiran and takes an arm. He levers Kiran to his feet. Isla and Nina help him out of the trench. At first Kiran resists then slumps, exhausted.

Isla feels his face and strokes his hair.

ISLA: He's freezing.

Jack places his coat around Kiran's shoulders.

ISLA: Thank you.

JACK: Let's get back. *(Nodding to Nina)* Pick up that
        torch, will you? It might be useful. Those   70

clouds are about to block the moon. Watch
out for tree roots.

Nina kneels down and scoops the torch up.

NINA: It's glowing.

JACK: That's what torches do.

NINA: But . . . glowing like it's breathing. Brighter   75
then dimmer.

Nina shows the torch to Jack.

NINA: *(The torch is dim)* Look. *(It brightens then dims)*

JACK: Just needs new batteries. C'mon, lead the
way, will you?

*Jack sets off with Kiran, taking most of his friend's
weight.*

JACK: It's not easy lugging this heavy lump about.   80
He's still out of it.

ISLA: Kiran? Are you okay?

JACK: *(Puffing)* He's out of it . . . just a dead weight.
Where's Tank when you need him?

NINA: It's getting brighter.   85

ISLA: Brilliant. Soon be morning, then.

NINA: *(Trembling)* No . . . I mean the torchlight is
getting brighter. Much brighter. The beam
goes for miles. *(She swings the torch towards
Jack)* See?   90

JACK: Not now you've blasted it in my eyes!

NINA: *(To Jack)* Sorry. It's hard to think straight. I'm
scared. And freezing. My jacket is ruined. I
can't feel my toes. Can't you go any faster?

31

JACK: *(Sarcastically)* Yeah. I'll just strap on some   95
bats and fly back. Or maybe you could click
your designer ruby slippers together three
times?

NINA: Suede boots, actually.

*They walk on, saying nothing. Nina is spooked by **nocturnal** animal noises.*

ISLA: *(Softly to Kiran)* Won't be long.   100

NINA: Good because I am seriously freaked.

A blood-curdling screech fills the air. Nina starts to run.

ISLA: *(Calling after her)* It's an owl. Just a barn owl.

NINA: *(Stopping)* A barn owl? Where's the barn?
There's no barn!

ISLA: The chalet is a barn conversion. It should   105
be close by.

JACK: We're not out of the woods yet.

Jack is struggling to hold on to Kiran who is trying to shake free.

NINA: Never will be if he carries on like this.

ISLA: Calm down, Kiran. You'll hurt yourself.

JACK: And me.   110

Jack lets Kiran go. Kiran stares at Jack blankly then turns to face Nina.

NINA: Isla. Don't take this the wrong way. *(Turning the torch on Kiran)* What if . . . your boyfriend's a zombie? Look at his dead eyes. Definitely

zombie eyes. *(Stumbling back)* I know it –
he's gonna eat my brains.   115

JACK: Just a quick snack then.

*Kiran approaches Nina who is shaking so much
she drops the torch.*

NINA: Just don't eat my boots.

*Kiran picks up the torch and aims it at the sky. A
thin, intense beam lights up the mist that drifts
around them.*

*Silence falls. The nocturnal sounds suddenly stop.
All is still. The torch goes out.*

NINA: *(Fed up)* Great. Now we can't see a thing.

JACK: You've got a mobile phone, right?

NINA: I'll call the police.   120

JACK: No, don't. *(Pause)* Just turn it on. The screen
will help us see where we're going.

NINA: Good idea.

*Nina pulls out her mobile phone. Suddenly an
intense, pulsating beam shines down on the
woods in front of the friends.*

JACK: *(To Kiran)* What have you done?

*Jack shakes Kiran's shoulders. Kiran drops to his
knees. He is coming out of the trance.*

KIRAN: A man in the wilderness asked this of me,   125
'How many strawberries grow in the sea?'
I answered him as I thought good,
'As many red herrings as swim in the wood.'

JACK:	What have you done?	
KIRAN:	I don't know . . . don't know . . . don't . . .	130
ISLA:	*(Hugging him)* It's okay.	

The beam is swooping closer.

NINA:	We're safe. That's from a helicopter. I know it is.	
JACK:	What can you hear, Nina?	
NINA:	*(Puzzled)* Nothing.	135
JACK:	Nothing is bad.	
NINA:	Is it?	
JACK:	No rotor blades.	

Kiran staggers to his feet and looks up. He hums the tune to 'Oranges and Lemons'. This spooks Isla.

JACK:	That thing up there is no chopper.	
KIRAN:	*(Mumbling)* 'Here comes the candle to light you to bed.'	140
ISLA:	Kiran?	
KIRAN:	*(Shouting)* 'Here comes a chopper to chop off your head!'	
ISLA:	You're scaring me, Kiran.	145
KIRAN:	*(Faintly to Isla)* Run.	
ISLA:	What?	
KIRAN:	*(Back to his senses)* Run!	

All four friends start to run from the beam that is searching Wulder Woods.

Blackout.

Scene 2

The edge of Wulder Woods, close to the field.

Kiran and Isla are pushing through the undergrowth together while Nina and Jack follow urgently behind. All are exhausted.

KIRAN: *(Stopping to look back)* My torch.

ISLA: Leave it.

KIRAN: I need it.

ISLA: Come on. I'll buy you another.

KIRAN: You don't understand, Isla. It's special. Dad 5
gave it to me just before I left home. He
instructed me to look after it. **Reiterated** it.
He said the torch would help me get back.

ISLA: I can get you back. The field is not far.

KIRAN: I'm not leaving without my torch. 10

ISLA: You're crazy, Kiran.

JACK: *(Out of breath)* What's up?

ISLA: Kiran wants to retrace our steps.

JACK: See that full moon? It turns some people
bonkers. 15

KIRAN: My torch. *(Wildly)* I *need* my torch!

JACK: Calm down. I know exactly where your
precious torch is. That direction. I caught my
foot on it and smacked into a tree. Nearly
broke my neck. 20

KIRAN: *(Angrily)* Why leave it there?

JACK: Easy answer. *(Firmly)* I'm trying to get out of
this wood ASAP.

NINA: So am I. *(Tugging Kiran)* Let's go.

KIRAN: *(Striding towards Jack)* I'm going, all right.   25
Back for my torch.

NINA: *(Despairing)* Kiran!

JACK: *(Blocking Kiran's way)* I'll go.

There is a glow in the distance moving between the trees.

ISLA: That beam is so close.

JACK: I don't think it's after us, Isla. *(Pointing back)*   30
I reckon it's searching the clearing. I'm not
going that far. I'll be quick as I can. Just make
sure Zombie-Eyes stays with you.

Jack runs back the way he came. Nina turns on Kiran.

NINA: *(Blazing)* Your torch is so special it's worth
losing a friend for?   35

KIRAN: Jack will be fine.

NINA: I meant me. Kiran, you're so selfish!

ISLA: Nina.

NINA: Isla thinks that too. Selfish. Only she won't
say so to your face. She loves your precious   40
mind so much she forgives the rest of you.

ISLA: Nina, please. Not now.

NINA: *(Firmly to Kiran)* Your brain is bursting with
so-called important facts but the only fact
worth knowing is that you have someone   45
special like Isla beside you. She is so patient,
way more than me. Loyal to a fault. Like a
pet waiting for a scrap of attention.

(Coldly) Kiran, you act as if my best friend is
just another gadget of yours. Something   50
to switch off or put on standby when you
get bored. An accessory.

KIRAN: *(Mumbling, trying to think of a defence)* We all
have accessories. You're one to talk.

NINA: What's that supposed to mean? *(Irritated)*   55
Oh, I get it. Well, mine are just superficial
things. Clothes. Bags. Useless things. Dead
things. Things that money can buy but are
not worth it. I may be shallow but at least I
know I am! Isla gives you everything. Her   60
time. Love. Important things.

ISLA: Kiran is one of a kind. Different.

NINA: Odd. Your boyfriend's just odd.

KIRAN: *(To Isla)* Has Nina got a boyfriend?

ISLA: You know she hasn't.   65

KIRAN: *(To Nina)* Ask yourself why.

NINA: This isn't about me. I'm just telling you to
cherish the positives in your life. And not be
such a robot!

KIRAN: Have you finished?   70

NINA: I've only just star—

*Nina is caught in a narrow, pulsating beam. Her
movements become sluggish, as if stuck in treacle.
She slowly crouches from the intense light.*

ISLA: No!

*Isla runs towards Nina. Kiran stops Isla and holds
her close. Nina looks back at Isla, gripped by fear.*

NINA:	*(Shivering)* So . . . cold.
ISLA:	*(To Kiran)* What's happening to her?
KIRAN:	Not sure. 75
ISLA:	Nina, roll out of the beam!
NINA:	Trying. But . . . it's setting round me . . . *(confused)* . . . like concrete. *(Panicking)* Get me out of this stuff!

Isla strides forward for Nina. Kiran pulls her back.

KIRAN:	Don't touch the light. *Never* touch the light! 80
ISLA:	How do you know that?
KIRAN:	I just do.

The beam glows brighter.

NINA:	Light . . . too bright. *(Panicking)* Isla! I can't see you!
ISLA:	Nina! We're here! 85
NINA:	Where? *(Blindly)* Where are you?
ISLA:	In front of you . . .

Nina looks straight up, then at her friends, with fear in her eyes.

NINA:	Help m—

The beam swings up, taking Nina with it.

ISLA:	Nina!
KIRAN:	She's gone. 90
ISLA:	Tell me it's a dream.
KIRAN:	*(Fearful)* It's a nightmare.
JACK:	*(Racing up to his friends)* Where's Nina?

ISLA: *(Sobbing)* The beam . . .

KIRAN: . . . swung up . . .   95

ISLA: . . . took her.

Isla begins to run off. Jack throws the torch to Kiran.

JACK: Satisfied? I hope this was worth it!

Kiran runs after Isla.

KIRAN: *(Calling back)* Why couldn't you keep out of my business? Out of Wulder Woods.

JACK: Why? You're just like a crazy kid brother.   100
         I've always had to watch your back.

Jack runs.

KIRAN: Never asked you to!

JACK: Old habits die hard!

The narrow, blinding beam is back. Striking Jack.

KIRAN: No!

Caught in the light, Jack's movements slow. He can't help looking up and is dazzled. The trapped boy drops to his knees.

ISLA: Not Jack!   105

JACK: Suffocating . . . hard to breathe.

ISLA: Get up!

JACK: My legs! I . . . can't move.

Isla runs up to Kiran who grabs her hand, bringing her to a halt.

KIRAN: Isla! Stay back.

ISLA: Jack needs help. *(Isla sighs, feeling helpless)*   110
What now?

JACK: Just go!

ISLA: No way. *(To Kiran)* Kiran, do something!

The beam brightens. Jack crouches, covering his eyes.

KIRAN: Too late.

Isla breaks free and reaches out to Jack.

KIRAN: I said don't touch him!   115

*The beam swings up, taking Jack from sight.
Kiran stumbles to Isla who shakes with fear.*

ISLA: Jack's gone. *(Fired up)* Your friend has gone!
This is all your fault! What were you doing in
these woods? Looking for trouble?

KIRAN: Answers.

Kiran looks up to the night sky. Isla pushes him firmly.

ISLA: Go! Traipsing through creepy woods like   120
Hansel and Gretel is not my idea of fun!

KIRAN: They got out. So will we.

ISLA: *(Sarcastically)* Lucky us.

KIRAN: I'm sorry.

*They hurry to the edge of Wulder Woods, with
Kiran leading Isla. Suddenly he feels her stop.*

KIRAN: Keep going.   125

*Kiran looks round to see the narrow beam is back.
Isla is lit up, apart from her right hand which is out
of the beam.*

ISLA: *(Surprised)* It's got me.

Kiran pulls Isla's right hand with both his own.

KIRAN: I've got you.

ISLA: Don't let it take me!

KIRAN: I won't.

ISLA: *(Terrified)* Kiran!   130

KIRAN: Hold tight.

*Kiran hauls on Isla's hand but the beam slowly
widens until it lights up Kiran's hands.*

ISLA: Your hands.

*Kiran leans back, arms outstretched, straining to
avoid being sucked into the light.*

KIRAN: Such force!

ISLA: Kiran . . . *(in a halting voice)* it's lifting me . . .
no, crushing me . . .   135

KIRAN: I can do this!

ISLA: Promise?

KIRAN: I . . . I . . .

ISLA: You can't, can you?

Kiran goes silent.

ISLA: *(Breathlessly)* Let go.   140

KIRAN: Never!

ISLA: *(Crying)* Then I will.

KIRAN: No!

ISLA: Find me!

Isla releases her grip, the beam swings up and she is swept away. Her final desperate words echo in the woods.

Kiran sinks to the ground. Frustrated, he pounds the earth and looks up in utter despair.

KIRAN: I didn't let go, Isla. I'd never let go of you.   145
Never. You're part of me. Always will be.
(In pain) Always . . .

Blackout.

Scene 3

A corridor in the chalet.

Kiran enters from the car park, exhausted. He closes the door and leans heavily against it.

KIRAN: I'm safe! *(Wearily)* I caused the grief but I'm the one who gets to walk away. *(Angrily)* They shouldn't have followed me! It wasn't worth it.

Kiran pulls out the half-brooch.

KIRAN: Nor was this junk. I found you but lost my   5
friends. My Isla! Why did I go there? What was so special about Wulder Woods? *(Frustrated)* I couldn't help myself.

Kiran shuffles up the corridor towards his room. He accidentally steps on the pizza box.

KIRAN: *(Sarcastically)* Oh great!

Bending, he picks up the pizza box and stands – holding the box – looking for a bin.

KIRAN: No bin. No friends . . .   10

MR GRANT: No wandering in the corridors at night, Kiran. I didn't expect to see you on my rounds.

Kiran turns to see Mr Grant wearing neatly ironed, striped pyjamas. Mr Grant points to the pizza box.

MR GRANT: Hungry?

KIRAN: Er, no.   15

MR GRANT: Moonlighting as a pizza-delivery boy, are you?

KIRAN:	I just found it. I was on my way to the bathroom.
MR GRANT:	*(Suspiciously)* In your coat?
KIRAN:	*(Floundering)* The heating's off. It's cold in this chalet. 20
MR GRANT:	And you really want me to believe that?
KIRAN:	*(Tired and snappy)* I really want to visit the bathroom.
MR GRANT:	Fair enough. Hand that pizza box to me. 25

Kiran does so.

MR GRANT:	Did you happen to find it in the freezer by any chance? I noticed earlier that two had magically appeared. What's this one? *(Studying the cover)* Pepperoni and tuna. Unusual combination of toppings. 30

Kiran looks disgusted as Mr Grant lifts the lid.

MR GRANT:	Pieces missing. I see you've tried it.
KIRAN:	*(Shrugging)* Not really my taste. Prefer pasta.
MR GRANT:	*(Smiling)* Then I shall make sure it goes to a good home.

Kiran takes hold of the handle to his room.

MR GRANT:	*(Coughs)* The bathroom is that way. 35
KIRAN:	*(Nodding)* Sure. I get confused this late at night. *(Yawning)* Need my sleep.
MR GRANT:	Then the sooner you retire to bed the better. Off you pop.
KIRAN:	*(Smiling)* Night-night. 40

Kiran trudges to the bathroom.

MR GRANT: Kids.

*Mr Grant waits until Kiran has gone then smiles.
He opens the box and pulls out a slice of cold pizza.*

MR GRANT: They think I was born yesterday. *(He takes a
big bite)* Mmm . . . somewhat gritty.

Mr Grant exits.

Blackout.

Scene 4

*Early morning. The circular clearing in Wulder
Woods.*

*Kiran, Mr Grant and Tank approach the trench. Mr
Grant is animated.*

KIRAN: *(Wearily)* I told you, Mr Grant. I don't know
where the others are. I wish I did.

MR GRANT: Three empty seats at breakfast and you
know nothing about it?

KIRAN: Maybe they got homesick?   5

MR GRANT: *(Colder)* Maybe you're covering for them.
Sticking up for your friends is not a bad
thing, Kiran, but it's not always right.

KIRAN: *(Fed up)* I don't need a lecture.

MR GRANT: I'll come straight to the point then. You had   10
a coat on in the corridor last night,
apparently because it was cold. I checked
with the chalet warden. The boiler was on
all night. Set at nineteen degrees. Plenty
warm enough. So why the coat?   15

KIRAN: *(Searching for an excuse)* I put my coat on to look for Jack. He left the room after lights out.

MR GRANT: Oh? Finally the truth. And?

KIRAN: And you stopped me before I got to the door.   20

MR GRANT: *(Softly)* Kiran. I like you. I trust you. But, today, I can see the fear in your eyes. Isla . . . Nina . . . Jack . . . are in trouble, aren't they? Where are your three friends?

KIRAN: *(Voice breaking)* I don't know!   25

TANK: Kiran doesn't have friends.

KIRAN: *(Snapping)* Oh, and you do? Everyone's scared of you, Tank. We all know what your temper's like. The whole school creeps around you pretending to be nice.   30

TANK: *(Lunges)* Why yer —

KIRAN: *(Kiran dodges)* In case you do that. BOOM! Go off on one.

TANK: *(To Mr Grant)* Kiran thinks he's so clever. But I ain't stupid.   35

MR GRANT: I never said you were.

TANK: But yer do *think* I'm stupid.

MR GRANT: *(Surprised)* Why do you say that?

TANK: *(Softer)* Yer didn't want me on this trip because yer thought I'd stir up trouble. But   40
I watch documentaries on the television. History. Geography. How things are made. Whatever. An' they stick in my mind. *(Tapping his head)* It's all in here. But yer both think I'm thick just because I can't get it out on   45
paper.

MR GRANT:	I didn't come into teaching to write pupils off, Thomas. My job is to get the best out of everyone. Sometimes it takes a while to make a connection. This is a busy time of 50 year. All that marking, preparing for exams, parents' evenings. Not easy.
TANK:	Your choice to teach.
MR GRANT:	*(Brighter)* And I don't regret it.
TANK:	I'm here and the others are not, Mr Grant. 55 Don't that tell yer something?
MR GRANT:	It does. *(To Kiran)* And something tells me you are keeping secrets. I'm not the greatest fan of secrets. Or my pupils bunking off breakfast. Thomas, don't make a joke about 60 no one liking apricot jam. I'm not in the mood.
TANK:	My sisters love it. Until I stir the teapot with a jammy spoon. Proper winds 'em up.
MR GRANT:	*(Ignoring Tank)* This morning I've been 65 obliged to telephone the school. Currently, the headteacher is digesting the *wonderful* news that three pupils are missing. My pupils! So what *is* going on, Kiran?
KIRAN:	*(Sighing)* I don't know. 70
MR GRANT:	Think, please. You have ten seconds before I ring the headteacher again and hand the phone over for you to do some explaining. Or maybe I should call the police?
KIRAN:	*(Blurting out the words)* All I know is they 75 went into the woods and . . .
MR GRANT:	Go on.

47

TANK: How do yer know that?

KIRAN: I was with them.

MR GRANT: *(To Tank)* Quiet. I'll ask the questions. 80
(To Kiran) And what happened when you
reached the woods?

KIRAN: They disappeared.

MR GRANT: People don't just disappear.

KIRAN: People do! 85

MR GRANT: Don't play games with me, Kiran.

*Professor Anderson approaches the trench, visibly
upset. She gestures to the disturbed ground.*

PROFESSOR: Vandals. Who on earth would do something
so appalling?

MR GRANT: *(To Kiran)* What have you got to say?

KIRAN: Vandals **sacked** Rome back in the year 455. 90
I don't really think this was them.

Professor Anderson studies Kiran closely.

MR GRANT: *(Rolling his eyes)* Vandalism as in mindless
destruction. *(To Professor Anderson)* This boy
just admitted he was out here last night.

PROFESSOR: He didn't need to. Iron oxide and 95
aluminium silicate stains on his coat. Sports
shoes caked in dried red clay.

*Professor Anderson gestures to footprints in the
trench.*

MR GRANT: *(Pointing to Kiran's left shoe)* Show me the
sole. *(Kiran does)*

PROFESSOR:	No prizes for guessing there is a perfect 100 match.
KIRAN:	*(Searching for an excuse)* I was sleepwalking.
MR GRANT:	The professor and I weren't born yesterday, Kiran.
PROFESSOR:	*(Irritated)* Judging from the mass of prints, 105 you and several others have stomped all over the site. My site! Do you appreciate the **inordinate** amount of time it took to get permission to excavate here? This is a site of special historical significance. *(Upset)* And 110 you thought it fun to wreck the archaeology?
KIRAN:	Sorry. *(Pleading)* I was out of it.
TANK:	Stomping in it, yer mean.
PROFESSOR:	*(To Mr Grant)* Nina, Jack and Isla. I assume they too are responsible? 115
TANK:	They've bunked off.
MR GRANT:	*(To Professor Anderson, apologetically)* It seems those three pupils are missing.
PROFESSOR:	Missing?
MR GRANT:	The chalet warden is out looking for them. 120
PROFESSOR:	And the police?
MR GRANT:	I dare say it's coming to that. I was hoping all three might . . .

Mr Grant sees Tank step into the trench.

MR GRANT:	Get out of there!
TANK:	Hey, Prof. See down here . . . where the soil 125 was dug up last night? There's something just here. *(He kneels)* A metal object.

49

Professor Anderson joins Tank.

PROFESSOR: You're right.

TANK: Needs taking out carefully like they do on
TV. Feels loose. Can I? 130

PROFESSOR: The soil layers have been destroyed. The
artefact is no longer *in situ*. *(Sighs)* What's
the harm?

*She nods and Tank starts easing out the other half
of the broken brooch.*

PROFESSOR: Gently does it.

Tank lifts the half-brooch free.

PROFESSOR: *(Surprised)* You have a light touch – and a 135
real talent.

TANK: *(Tank gestures to Mr Grant and Kiran)* Tell that
to them.

*Mr Grant is fiddling uneasily with his mobile
phone.*

PROFESSOR: This find must be tagged and **conserved**.
(Scowling at Kiran) It's hard to assess the age 140
because of the destruction of the soil layers.

KIRAN: I said I'm sorry.

PROFESSOR: *(To Tank)* Normally I'd use the relative
placement of soil deposits to assign dates
using the Law of Superposition. 145

TANK: Normally what?

PROFESSOR: *(Patiently)* The deeper the soil layer, the
earlier the date. This find is difficult to date

anyway. The markings are nothing I
recognise. Not Saxon.   150

*Professor Anderson places the half-brooch on the
finds table. Kiran turns away and glances at his
own half-brooch.*

MR GRANT: I'm going to have to make that phone call.

Mr Grant taps his mobile phone.

PROFESSOR: Police?

Mr Grant nods.

KIRAN: No. Not yet, Mr Grant. Please.

*Mr Grant looks over at Kiran, finger poised to
make the call.*

MR GRANT: What's in your left hand?

KIRAN: Nothing. *(Resigned)* Something I found.   155

MR GRANT: *(Unimpressed)* Really? Let me guess – you
found it here in this trench.

Kiran holds up his half of the brooch.

KIRAN: *(Nods)* It's similar to the object Tank just
found. I think both halves fit together to
make a metal brooch.   160

PROFESSOR: And you discovered this artefact last night?

KIRAN: Yes. In the dark.

PROFESSOR: In my trench! *(Angrily)* Kiran, you had no
right to dig it up.

KIRAN: I had no choice.   165

PROFESSOR: 'Finders keepers' might apply in a school

playground, Kiran, but not on a professional archaeological dig. Mr Grant, this is a serious breach of my rules. In less than twenty-four hours your pupils have run riot. Who is in charge? Them or you? 170

MR GRANT: *(Furiously)* Me.

PROFESSOR: You have three pupils still free to create mischief. Without wishing to be rude, isn't it time you made that call? 175

Professor Anderson thrusts her hand out to claim Kiran's find.

TANK: Hey! The vandals are invading again!

Everyone turns to look. Isla, Jack and Nina are striding woodenly into the clearing. Each stares ahead, wide-eyed.

TANK: What's up with them? Jack. Nina. Isla. Your eyes. Whoa – freaky!

MR GRANT: Where have you been? *(Lowering his phone)* I was about to call the police. 180

The friends move closer, puppet-like. They stop as one, staring at Kiran.

MR GRANT: Answer me!

KIRAN: They can't. Something happened to them in Wulder Woods last night.

MR GRANT: Oh? *(Irritated)* Do tell.

KIRAN: One by one the beam got them. 185

MR GRANT: *(Curtly)* What beam?

KIRAN: A narrow beam of light **emanating** from the

sky. From space for all I know. We all tried to run out of the woods. Thought we'd got far enough away from it. *(Pause)* Nina was first, 190 then Jack. Isla . . . Isla was pulled from my hand. *(Choking)* I tried to hold her . . . protect her . . . but . . .

MR GRANT: Enough. Mysterious beams in the woods? Next, you'll expect me to believe in fairies 195 at the bottom of the garden.

TANK: I saw a documentary about that.

MR GRANT: Fairies?

TANK: Strange beams of light. Turned out it was a secret section of the army that not even 200 the army knew about – and they were testing new weapons. High-grade military lasers.

MR GRANT: I must congratulate you both on your vivid imaginations. These three friends of yours have some explaining to do. 205

Professor Anderson feels something is wrong. She approaches Nina.

PROFESSOR: Nina! *(Kindly)* Speak to me. This is Professor Anderson.

Nina looks at Professor Anderson coldly. Professor Anderson steps back, suddenly afraid.

TANK: Who'd have thought field trips could be this cool!

Isla, Jack and Nina stop in front of Kiran and the others.

KIRAN: Isla. It's me. Kiran. 210

Isla stares blankly at him.

MR GRANT: Professor. Their eyes. Blank.

Kiran runs forward.

MR GRANT: Kiran, stay back!

KIRAN: But she'll listen to me.

MR GRANT: Back! *(To Professor Anderson)* Chances are
it's drugs.   215

TANK: *(Mocking)* Or glue.

PROFESSOR: *(Seriously)* Or both.

KIRAN: Don't you get it? It's the beam! Won't anyone
listen to me? My friends were taken away and
some *thing* did this to them.   220

TANK: Sucked their brains out!

Tank picks up a stick.

KIRAN: *(To Tank)* What are you thinking?

TANK: I'm thinking vampires . . . zombies . . .

*Isla starts walking closer to Kiran. Jack then Nina
follow. Tank raises the stick. Kiran wrestles it from
Tank.*

KIRAN: Don't hurt her, Tank. Or . . .

TANK: *(Pushing Kiran to the ground)* Don't waste   225
your breath.

MR GRANT: I get it. *(Groaning)* Now I understand what's
going on. This is a wind-up. *(To Professor
Anderson)* A childish prank that's gone too far!

PROFESSOR: I'm not sure.   230

Jack grabs Kiran and starts to drag him off.

KIRAN: Get off me!

MR GRANT: Joke's over!

Isla and Nina also take hold of Kiran. Their grip is strong.

MR GRANT: Let me remind you, this is a geography trip *not* a drama class.

KIRAN: *(To Jack)* You're hurting me.   235

Kiran is pushed against the finds table. It tips over, spilling boxes and finds on the ground. Unable to stop himself, Kiran snatches the other half of the brooch. In the confusion, no one notices.

PROFESSOR: Please. Listen to your teacher! *(She looks at Mr Grant for support)* Mr Grant, you're obviously a man of high principles – do something.

MR GRANT: *Am I?* *(Keen to impress)* Yes – I am. All four of you – go back to the chalet! I'm in no   240
mood for this charade!

Kiran is pulled closer to the trees.

PROFESSOR: No one appears to be listening.

MR GRANT: *(Irritated)* I'll make them listen. The chalet is that way! You're all going in the wrong direction!   245

Mr Grant strides forward.

MR GRANT: Come on you lot. Back to the chalet. Now!

Kiran is dragged into the trees. He struggles but cannot break free.

KIRAN: *(Scared)* Mr Grant!

TANK:	*(Frowning)* Maybe Kiran is in trouble?
MR GRANT:	Oh, he is. Big trouble when I've finished with him. 250
KIRAN:	*(Distant)* Tank!

Tank strides forward. Professor Anderson takes his arm.

PROFESSOR:	Don't get involved. *(To Mr Grant)* I'd like this student to stay here.
MR GRANT:	Thomas? *(Surprised)* Really? I suppose he's one less worry. 255
PROFESSOR:	I'm sure he'll be most useful. What with all this **devastation** to clear up.
MR GRANT:	*(Distractedly)* Have him.

Mr Grant stares at the trees beyond the clearing. He shivers.

MR GRANT:	This place creeps me out.
PROFESSOR:	You get used to it. *(With a sympathetic smile)* 260 It has its attractions.

Mr Grant walks slowly away from the professor and glances at the woods.

MR GRANT:	*(Turning round)* My apologies, Professor. Twenty years of teaching leads to what? Chaos. Anarchy.
PROFESSOR:	History is littered with groups challenging 265 authority.
MR GRANT:	*(Grim)* Firm. Fair. Consistent. Sense of humour. That is – was – my usual policy.

PROFESSOR: Mine too. You ought to check those jokers
are doing what you've said.   270

Mr Grant nods and exits the way the others left.

TANK: He's losing it.

PROFESSOR: I'm sure Mr Grant has it all in hand.

TANK: Yer reckon? I s'pose he's one of the better
teachers. One that listens. I try not to play
him up. *(Smiles)* Too much.   275

PROFESSOR: As long as you don't play me up we'll get
along hunky-dory. Let's begin by sorting out
the finds table. Everything *was* in
chronological order. Now it's all over the
place.   280

TANK: All over the mud, yer mean.

*Happy to be the centre of attention, Tank rights
the finds table.*

TANK: So what is the earliest thing you've found in
this trench?

*Professor Anderson retrieves a piece of flint and
places it at one end of the finds table.*

PROFESSOR: This. Doesn't look much, does it?

TANK: A bit of stone.   285

PROFESSOR: A **Neolithic** leaf-shaped flint arrowhead.
Sharp as the day it was chipped. Sliced my
thumb when I pulled it out. *(Holds up her
thumb, smiles)* Still got the scar. I'd say most
of the finds are Saxon. I expected that.   290
Wulder Woods has a Saxon name.

TANK: Named after a sky god. Uller or something.

PROFESSOR: *(Impressed)* How did you . . .?

TANK: Yer said it yesterday. I do listen – might not
look like it.   295

PROFESSOR: Then you'll go places. *(Smiling)* Maybe as far
as I have. Peru. Bolivia. India. Egypt . . .

TANK: Furthest I've been from home is here.

PROFESSOR: We all have to start somewhere.

*Tank and Professor Anderson walk around,
carefully picking things up.*

Blackout.

Act Three

Scene 1

Wulder Woods.

Jack, Nina and Isla drag Kiran through the thick undergrowth. He is tired and scared.

KIRAN: Leave me alone.

Kiran slips out of his coat and staggers backwards, falling to the ground.

His three friends bend silently over him.

KIRAN: What happened? Who did this to you? *(Petrified)* Answer me! Say something!

Isla jerks straight, her head tipping back.

KIRAN: Isla?

Jack and Nina also straighten.

The three friends begin to speak in time, all together, and a single, strange voice comes out. It is alien but clear and soft.

VOICE: Kor-daksh isk mau.   5

KIRAN: Isla. Is this a joke?

VOICE: Kor-daksh isk mau.

KIRAN: *(Looking at Isla's eyes)* But how . . .? That's not Isla.

VOICE: Kor-daksh isk mau.   10

KIRAN: *(Turning to Jack)* Not Jack.

VOICE: Kor-daksh isk mau.

KIRAN: *(Staring at Nina)* Not Nina.

VOICE: Kor-daksh isk mau.

KIRAN: What are you . . . it . . . saying? 15

All three friends close their mouths and stare at Kiran. Jack studies the coat in his hands as if he has never seen one before.

KIRAN: You're holding my coat, Jack. You've seen it a million times before. What's happened to you? *(To himself)* Not answering. Think this through, Kiran. Be logical.

Kiran pauses, thinking hard.

KIRAN: They're acting possessed. Outta their minds. 20 That's it! *(Aloud)* Whatever it is you are, I know you've taken over my friends. They're important to me. I care about them.

Kiran faces Isla. Gets close.

KIRAN: And I *really* care about Isla. What are you? And what are you doing in her mind? If you 25 hurt her I'll . . .

The voice says nothing. Kiran takes a defiant pose.

KIRAN: How do I know Isla still exists? That you haven't wiped her memories and personality? Prove she's still okay. *(Angry)* Prove it!

Isla collapses. Kiran runs forward and holds her close.

ISLA: *(Weakly)* Kiran? 30

KIRAN: Isla?

ISLA: *(Barely nodding)* Yes . . . me . . . Isla.
Headache. Sleepy.

Isla's eyes close.

KIRAN: You're back.

Kiran is forcing back tears, rocking her. Suddenly he sees Jack pull out the torch.

KIRAN: Give that torch to me, Jack. You don't need   35
it. Or maybe you do. *(Thinks quickly)* Of
course! It's a beacon. Used to attract the
beam.

Jack studies it closely. Kiran puts Isla down gently and crosses to Jack.

KIRAN: Jack. We've always shared things. But not
now. That's mine.   40

Kiran tries to snatch the torch but Jack lifts it straight up. The torch is now pointing to the sky.

KIRAN: I want it back! That's not a good idea!

Kiran tugs on Jack's outstretched arm but Jack is too strong. The torch begins glowing brightly straight through the overhanging branches.

Suddenly Kiran is bathed in intense bright light. The beam is back. Kiran looks up.

KIRAN: Incredible! *(Awestruck)* A spacecraft. Can't be.
(He glances up again) It is.

Dazzled, Kiran slowly drops to a crouch. Isla wakens and stands. She begins to walk towards the beam. Her eyes are now blank.

KIRAN: Isla! Run.

Kiran cries despairingly as he sees her blank look.

KIRAN: No! Not again! Why can't you leave her   45
alone? *(Staring straight up)* Leave all my
friends alone. I know what you want. I'm not
stupid. You want me. You . . . want . . . me!

*The beam swings upwards and Kiran is gone. Isla
is left standing motionless in the gloom. Jack and
Nina lurk nearby, all still as statues.*

Blackout.

Scene 2

The circular clearing in Wulder Woods.

*Professor Anderson is busy covering the finds
table with plastic sheeting. Mr Grant runs towards
her.*

MR GRANT: Professor Anderson?

PROFESSOR: *(Surprised to see him)* Yes? Won't be a tick. Just
covering this in case it rains. Did you see the
lightning?

MR GRANT: It's so dark and dense in there I couldn't   5
see a thing.

PROFESSOR: The others?

MR GRANT: *(Embarrassed)* I'm dense too. Shouldn't have
been that hard to track them down but I
guess I got lost.   10

PROFESSOR: Easily done. Any paths that existed are long
overgrown. If your pupils keep walking they

will either end up out of the woods or back here, like you did.

TANK: Nice walk, sir?   15

MR GRANT: Very nice, thank you, Thomas.

TANK: Yer ripped yer coat.

MR GRANT: *(Sees the tear. Groans)* Jenny will be delighted.

PROFESSOR: Your wife?

MR GRANT: My dog. It'll go in her bed. *(Pause)* I'm —   20

TANK: Divorced. *(Laughing)* Everyone knows that. Are yer married, Professor?

PROFESSOR: To my work.

TANK: What a shame, eh, Mr Grant?

MR GRANT: *(Firmly to Tank)* I'm sure you've got work to   25
do.

Tank begins sieving soil into a tray.

PROFESSOR: Actually *(quietly)* I do have some days off.

MR GRANT: *(Brightens)* Oh, right. So do I.

PROFESSOR: You're a teacher.

MR GRANT: *(Rolls eyes up)* All those holidays, I know.   30

PROFESSOR: Compensation for putting up with all those kids.

MR GRANT: Do you have kids?

PROFESSOR: What kind of a question is that? *(Mr Grant looks embarrassed)* It's okay. I'm on my   35
own – no kids. I spend most of my time alone, especially here. So it's nice to have company. Thomas has been a real boon.

MR GRANT: Glad to hear it.

PROFESSOR:	*(Quietly to Mr Grant)* Perhaps you should join me sometime?
MR GRANT:	*(Flustered)* Really?
PROFESSOR:	Really.
MR GRANT:	I'd like that. Are you —?

Mr Grant's mobile rings. He answers it.

MR GRANT:	Yes. Yes. I hear you. It's almost under control. I am doing my best. I will. Goodbye.
PROFESSOR:	Bad news?
MR GRANT:	*(Regretfully)* Bad timing . . .

Mr Grant strides to the trees lining the clearing.

MR GRANT:	It's imperative I get to the bottom of this mess. This trip is a total disaster.

*Professor Anderson looks at him with **compassion**.*

PROFESSOR:	Not total.
MR GRANT:	No?
PROFESSOR:	No.

The professor scrawls on a scrap of paper and hands it to him. Mr Grant reads it then looks surprised. For a moment he smiles, then cools as he turns to where the pupils disappeared into the woods.

PROFESSOR:	I'll come with you.
MR GRANT:	*(Pleased)* Then we all have to go. *(Glancing at Tank)* Put that down, Thomas, and come with us.

TANK: *(Grumbling)* Make up your mind.

MR GRANT: *(To himself)* To think I used to love weekends.

They all exit.

Blackout.

Scene 3

Inside the alien spacecraft.

Kiran crouches in a large, open space with a domed roof and curved walls. There is a gentle humming noise. Kiran clutches his head.

KIRAN: Headache . . . **ice cream headache**!

Kiran staggers upright. Clears his head.

KIRAN: *(Joking)* Welcome aboard the *Starship Enterprise. (Gazing around in near-darkness)* No one here. If you can hear me, answer this – what do you want with me? *(Silence)*   5 It'd help if you put the lights on.

*A panel slides back to reveal a circular **indentation** in the wall, glowing blue. The room is slightly brighter now. Kiran makes out strange markings on the walls.*

KIRAN: *(Surprised)* Thank you.

Curious, Kiran goes to a marking.

KIRAN: Looks familiar.

He touches the marking but pulls away, as if it is hot.

KIRAN: Feels familiar. Like a book you once read as a child. Bringing back . . . lost memories. *(Clutching his head)* I see a **supernova** but it's so close, so bright. *(Pause)* Now it's fading and I feel cold. *(Shivering)* Cold as loneliness. Cold as . . . death. 10

Kiran drops to his knees, hands over his eyes. The moment passes. He looks at the glowing, blue indentation then staggers over to it.

KIRAN: What is this? Not just a light. Maybe it's studying me. Watching what I do next. *(Swinging round)* I'm not scared of you! Whatever it is you are *(half-laugh)* I'm petrified. 15

Kiran realises he is now holding both halves of the brooch. He holds them up close together in front of the indentation.

KIRAN: Two pieces of a bigger puzzle. Putting them together feels right. But you know that. You want me to do this. *(Sighing)* So do I. 20

The two halves join perfectly together. An unseen force shunts Kiran forward and the whole brooch slots into the indentation. A perfect fit.

Blue light lasers through pinpricks in the brooch to project stars onto the roof.

KIRAN: Awesome. A galaxy of stars. *(Kiran wanders to the centre of the room and gazes at the blue stars above)* Blue stars. I've seen these before.

Kiran winces, head hurting.

KIRAN: When? Hard to think back. I was at my 25
house. Where? Upstairs. Dad's office. Yes!
Dad shut down the computer. Didn't want
me to see something . . . a map. What of? A
galaxy. *(Looking up and remembering)* This
galaxy? It's beautiful. 30

Jack appears in the spacecraft. Then Nina and Isla.

Kiran is in the centre of them, wary of their wide-eyed staring.

Still taken over by something unknown, Jack, Nina and Isla begin to speak together in its alien voice.

VOICE: Ag Kax Keeeeran.

KIRAN: Your words are strange.

VOICE: Keeeran. *(Pause)* Kiran.

KIRAN: *(Gasping)* You know my name. Yes. I am
Kiran. 35

VOICE: *(Haltingly)* I . . . am . . . the . . . Finder . . .

KIRAN: *(With disbelief)* You're not making sense.

VOICE: *(Less hesitant)* You . . . are the . . .
Foundling. *(Pause)*

(Smoothly) The Finder has travelled far. 40
From the dawn of this . . . your universe.
Searching. Finding.

KIRAN: *(Incredulously)* Thirteen point seven billion
light years away?

VOICE: Time and distance mean nothing to the 45
Finder.

KIRAN: You're an alien. Not of my world. You say
you came all that way to find me, a human.

I'm just a boring boy from a boring school in
a boring town somewhere that's too boring 50
to mention. So you wasted your time. Go
and find someone else more interesting.

VOICE: The Finder is your Guardian. The search is
over.

*The projected blue stars blink and disappear. One
star is left. A single beam of light shines from the
brooch.*

KIRAN: I get it. *(Pointing upwards)* This distant star 55
is where you originate from.

VOICE: You originate. We originate.

KIRAN: That's crazy. If that's true, how did I get here
from there?

*The single star bursts into a dazzling bright light
and then fades, like a firework.*

KIRAN: *(Gasps)* A supernova. 60

VOICE: An unimaginable power blasted you. You
became lost and drifted, unconscious,
through space. In time you woke, here, with
no memory of the past. And took human
form for your protection. 65

KIRAN: No! You're lying.

*Kiran runs to the recess and yanks out the brooch.
The halves are now fused into one piece.*

KIRAN: What you say is pure **fabrication**. I was
born on the seventeenth of December here
on Earth. I have parents and grandparents,
uncles and aunts, cousins. My mum and 70

dad run a holiday cottage in the middle of nowhere.

VOICE: Your parents are the Witnesses.

KIRAN: Witnesses to what?

VOICE: Hear their words.   75

Isla, Jack and Nina drop their heads. The room fills with countryside sounds as if open to the outdoors.

The lighting changes and a three-dimensional image appears showing Kiran's mum and dad standing together facing him. A recording plays.

MUM: Kiran?

DAD: Kiran?

KIRAN: *(Shuddering in recognition)* Mum . . . Dad! Is that really you?

Kiran gingerly walks round his parents, unsure whether to reach out and touch them. They do not follow his movements but always look straight ahead.

MUM: *(Sadly)* Kiran. What we're about to say might   80
seem unbelievable. It was to us.

DAD: Son. Fourteen years ago your mum and I witnessed something that would change our lives forever. Now it's time you knew what we found.   85

MUM: So you know the truth. *(Tearfully)* About yourself. And us.

DAD: Last night we met the Finder. We knew some *thing* would come. To use us to convince you of the truth of what it tells you.   90

KIRAN: What truth?

MUM: This is some kind of recording. We don't
understand how it works. The Finder is
enveloping us as we speak. Guess that won't
make much sense. We can't see or hear you. 95
But we know you can see and hear us.

DAD: *(Fearfully)* It's nearly time.

KIRAN: Time for what? Mum? Why are you crying?
(Pause) She can't answer.

DAD: One night we were strolling in the field 100
alongside our garden and saw an unearthly
glow in the sky. We were astonished.

MUM: Excited.

DAD: Your mum thought it was the Northern
Lights. It was so energised and beautiful. 105
The glow came closer, shrinking, becoming
brighter.

MUM: Swirling and shimmering like a silver-blue
sea mist.

DAD: All at once we were enveloped by it. 110

MUM: It felt so odd. As if every atom in us was
vibrating in time to another being.

DAD: We felt as if the mist were alive.

MUM: We were alive.

DAD: But we felt its weakness, fear. 115

MUM: The mist was warming itself.

DAD: Hugging us for strength.

MUM: Communicating.

DAD: Needing love. A place to rest after a
wearying, energy-sapping journey. 120

MUM: Shrinking further, it took human form.

DAD: Shimmering like a beautiful angel.

MUM: Our angel.

DAD: *(Still amazed after all these years)* An innocent, newborn babe. 125

MUM AND DAD: *(Happily)* You.

KIRAN: *(Barely able to speak)* You're talking about me?

MUM: I wrapped you up and we brought you into the warm. You were so light. 130

DAD: You were light.

MUM: We named you Kiran. Our 'ray of light'.

DAD: *(Tenderly)* Kiran. We knew from the start we only had you for a little time. It was impossible to stop time counting down. 135

KIRAN: *(Remembering)* I saw a clock in the corner of the screen, Dad.

DAD: I set up a computer program. We had to know what time we had left. That's why I kept hold of that old computer. *(Chuckles)* 140
You were always so desperate for me to throw it out. All your life we have watched an unfeeling clock counting down too fast.

MUM: Ticking off each precious family moment. We know when you see this recording of us . . . 145
(sorrowfully) the clock will be in its final moments.

KIRAN: No.

DAD: Soon it will stop.

KIRAN:	NO!	150

MUM: *(Upset)* I'll always be your mum. I made a promise that first night. To pick you up when you fall, caress your cheek and hold you tight. Help you learn and grow and love.

DAD: And I'm your dad, who shows you the stars 155 and watches over you as you sleep peacefully in bed, chasing the nightmares away. Your daft dad always embarrassing you in front of your girlfriend.

MUM: The doctors said we would never have a 160 child. They were wrong. We had you, Kiran. From the start, you lit up our lives with your energy and innocence. And from the start you were learning so much, so quickly.

DAD: But now there is so much more for you to 165 explore. To discover.

MUM: *(Crying)* Only you can say if we did a good job.

KIRAN: You did. You do!

MUM: *(Blowing a kiss)* Love you. Wherever you go. 170

DAD: Love you always, son. Whatever you do.

KIRAN: *(Upset)* Love you too.

The image shudders.

KIRAN: Don't go!

The image breaks up, then fades. Kiran wipes away tears with his sleeve.

KIRAN: *(Hurting)* Finder? Take me back. I need to 175

see my parents. You have no right to keep
me or my friends here. Let us all go. Now!

*Isla, Jack and Nina raise their heads and speak as
one.*

VOICE: The Witnesses you call your parents both
know you are not of their kind. The Finder
thanks them. They are young and do not   180
understand. But you are almost as old as time.

KIRAN: I'm fourteen.

VOICE: Your earthly body is temporary. A protective
shell you can cast off soon. Your friends will
return to Wulder Woods.   185

KIRAN: And what of me?

VOICE: *(Serenely)* You return to the **cosmos** in your
original form.

KIRAN: What will I be?

VOICE: Found.   190

KIRAN: *(Interested)* Are there more like me?

VOICE: Many become lost in space. In time all will
be found.

KIRAN: Do I have to go?

VOICE: You cannot stay.   195

KIRAN: The ticking clock. *(Accepting)* I understand.
Part of me has always felt as if I am an
outsider. But you're saying I never was. I've
always belonged somewhere. Here.

VOICE: And there.   200

KIRAN: I'm not ready to go. Let me say farewell to
my friends. To Isla.

Jack, Nina and Isla come to their senses. For a moment they clutch their heads, confused. Kiran rushes around them all, checking they are all right.

KIRAN: Jack. How are you feeling?

JACK: Like I've been run over by a heavy light. What happened?   205

KIRAN: It's a long story.

NINA: Don't bother. Just tell me my brains haven't been sucked out.

JACK: *(Smiling)* Hard to tell.

KIRAN: You'll be fine. The headache goes soon   210
enough. Isla? Are you okay?

ISLA: I've felt better.

Kiran hugs Isla tight, unwilling to let go.

KIRAN: Back in Wulder Woods, I held on to you as long as I could. The beam was too strong. I thought I'd lost you forever.   215

ISLA: But it was only a moment ago.

KIRAN: It was yesterday.

JACK: *(Rubbing his throat)* Time flies when you're having fun. Anyone else got a sore throat?

All murmur in agreement as Kiran faces them.

KIRAN: Your minds and vocal cords were   220
borrowed.

NINA: Gross.

JACK: By what?

KIRAN: The Finder. An alien **entity**. It wished to speak to me.   225

NINA: What? *(Mocking)* And this is its spaceship?

KIRAN: Yes. *(Serious)* Some kind of alien transport
        vehicle. Capable of incredible speeds. Able to
        travel across our universe in fourteen years,
        seven months and, I guess, four days.   230

JACK: Trust you to know that.

KIRAN: My age.

NINA: If it wanted a chat, why didn't it just ring you
        up? *(Kiran shrugs)* Am I meant to believe this
        alien-being thingy has a supercharged   235
        spaceship *(sarcastically)* but not a mobile
        phone?

KIRAN: Something like that.

JACK: So what's so special about you?

KIRAN: I'm not special. Just different.   240

ISLA: This is the most **surreal** thing ever to
        happen to us. We're chatting away like we're
        in the school canteen when we're actually in
        a **sinister** alien spacecraft. We could be
        heading anywhere.   245

KIRAN: The technology in here is obviously
        sophisticated. My guess is we're almost
        certainly shielded from detection – and still
        above Wulder Woods.

NINA: *(Mocking)* That's okay then. All we have to   250
        do is find a way out and jump without
        parachutes. The trees will break our fall.

JACK: And our legs.

ISLA: Kiran. Why did the Finder want to
        communicate with you? Not us.   255

KIRAN: Do you want me to lie? It would be easier.

ISLA: *(Hugging him)* We've always been honest with each other.

KIRAN: You want the truth. I'm not sure you're ready for it or I'm ready for it. 260

NINA: Why did it want you?

KIRAN: *(Struggling to find the words)* To tell me my time is running out.

ISLA: *(Shocked)* You're dying?

JACK: Don't be silly, Isla. 265

KIRAN: Sort of.

JACK: What?

ISLA: Kiran?

KIRAN: I'm not sure. Maybe the opposite.

JACK: *(Confused)* Being reborn? 270

KIRAN: Look, this isn't easy for me to explain.

NINA: Aliens. Spaceships. It's all gone weird. *(To Kiran)* You've gone weird. *(Panicking)* I've got to get out of here. Where's the door?

KIRAN: You'll get out soon, Nina. 275

ISLA: We all will.

KIRAN: No. *(Shakes his head)* Not me.

ISLA: No?

KIRAN: *(Pained)* I'm sorry, Isla.

ISLA: Sorry? What kind of a word is that? You're 280 coming with me. I won't let you stay on board. Nina's right. This place is weird. That Finder alien creep is messing with your mind too.

KIRAN: *(Shaking his head)* I have no choice, Isla.   285
The clock.

ISLA: What clock?

Kiran jolts, tightens. A tingling sensation fires through his body.

KIRAN: The clock has stopped.

Kiran steps forward and hugs Isla hard. He steps back.

A smile spreads over Kiran's face and he relaxes. All his tension is flowing out of him.

KIRAN: *(To Isla)* I'll never forget you.

Kiran hands Isla the fused brooch.

KIRAN: With this, you can remember me. It shows   290
where I came from. Where I'm going to.

ISLA: Kiran. What are you saying? You belong with us . . . with me!

KIRAN: Yes. *(Happily)* And the stars.

NINA: Your hands!   295

*Kiran sees his hands are slowly **disintegrating** into sparkling particles.*

KIRAN: It is time.

ISLA: *(**Distraught**)* Please stay with me.

KIRAN: *(Sorrowfully)* It is time.

ISLA: Jack. Make it stop.

JACK: I can't.   300

KIRAN: No one can.

ISLA: *(Desperately)* Then let me travel the stars with you. We belong together. *(Excited now)* Kiran, I can come with you. The Finder will let me. *(Looking around)* Won't you? Won't you? 305

KIRAN: See how I become light? Isla, it is *my* **destiny**.

JACK: *(Understands)* Farewell, my crazy friend.

NINA: Goodbye, Kiran.

ISLA: *(Crying)* I won't let you go. I promise.

KIRAN: You must. 310

ISLA: Never.

KIRAN: Isla, keep me in your heart.

ISLA: I love you, Kiran.

KIRAN: Love binds us all.

Kiran is fading. Isla reaches out with trembling fingertips.

ISLA: *(In wonder)* Star dust? 315

KIRAN: *(Murmuring)* Love . . .

ISLA: *(Crying)* Goodbye.

KIRAN: *(faintly)* . . . you.

Isla, Jack and Nina rush forward to hug their friend. But Kiran is now just a shimmering presence.

A second bright presence appears and the space glows an intense white.

Blackout.

Scene 4

The circular clearing in Wulder Woods.

Bathed in a beam of light, Isla, Jack and Nina find themselves on Earth, all hugging. The beam vanishes.

They look up at the hovering spacecraft. It flashes off at fantastic speed.

Meanwhile, Tank is busy looking at the finds table. He glances up to see Isla, Jack and Nina nearby.

TANK: Oh, back are yer? Had your fun? What did yer do to Kiran? Tie him to a tree?

ISLA: Gone. *(In shock)* My Kiran's gone.

TANK: Off with the fairies, eh?

JACK: *(Numbly)* Something like that.   5

TANK: All that zombie vampire stuff was good. Had me going for a bit. Not that I was scared. I don't do scared. *(Pause)* But yer took it too far.

NINA: What?   10

JACK: That's rich coming from you.

TANK: Dragging Kiran away like that. You freaked him. Kiran was out of his mind.

NINA: *(Quietly)* We all were.

TANK: *(Gesturing into the woods)* When are yer gonna let him go?   15

JACK: We already have.

ISLA: No! *(Upset)* I'll never let Kiran go.

> *Tank gives Isla a puzzled frown. Nina stares at Tank with a 'leave it' look.*

TANK: You lot were gone for ages. Better get some excuses ready. I've been thinking about this place. See this dip. Reminds me of a rugby game. *(Enthusiastically)* The penalty kicker presses the rugby ball into a pile of sand. And it makes a dip. Now, what if . . .   20

JACK: A giant rugby ball fell from the sky and landed here? Or how about an alien spacecraft?   25

TANK: *(Irritated)* Wind-up merchant!

NINA: *(Sharply)* Stop having a go at each other. Try being nice.   30

ISLA: Nina's right. *(Looking up)* Kiran said, 'Love binds us all.'

JACK: *(Nods)* We're only here once so let's make the most of it.

TANK: The prof says *I* can come back here when I want.   35

JACK: I meant something else, Tank.

ISLA: *(Sadly)* Someone else.

NINA: Has Kiran really gone? *(Looking up)* Odd how I feel lost without him.   40

ISLA: My . . . boyfriend left me.

JACK: Kiran had no choice.

NINA: *(Comforting)* He left you with memories. His poor parents.

ISLA: *(Suddenly bitter)* It's okay for them. They saw it coming and had time to adjust.   45

NINA: Should we tell the teachers what we know?

JACK: Best say nothing. We're in enough trouble as it is.

Mr Grant and Professor Anderson enter the clearing, after a tiring search.

MR GRANT: There you are! The **prodigal** children have returned.   50

JACK: *(Under his breath)* Three . . . two . . . one . . .

TANK: Boom!

MR GRANT: I told you all to go back to the chalet. But no. You thought you'd play hide and seek in   55 these wretched woods. I've ruined a perfectly good leather coat. The professor has wasted valuable time. And the headteacher is going crazy.

JACK: Did you see it?   60

MR GRANT: What?

JACK: Above Wulder Woods?

MR GRANT: If you think I'm going to play Twenty Questions . . .

NINA: The spacecraft!   65

MR GRANT: Let me get this right, Jack . . . Nina? You're asking me if I've seen an *alien* spacecraft?

JACK AND NINA: Yes.

MR GRANT: Everywhere I've looked today I've seen trees, trees and more trees . . . Did I   70 mention trees? But, funnily enough, no spacecraft. Not even up there.

PROFESSOR: Before you ask, I haven't seen anything either.

MR GRANT:	I hoped this trip might be a life-changing, uplifting experience. It's nothing short of a 75 disaster. I've got you lot to thank for that.
TANK:	*(Protesting)* I didn't do nothing.
MR GRANT:	For once – no – Thomas. You seem to be the only sensible one around here. What am I saying? **(Bemused)** I must be mad. 80
PROFESSOR:	Mr Grant, this field trip isn't over until you set off tomorrow afternoon. I am just as disappointed as you but I'm prepared to give your pupils a second chance. *If* everyone works together. 85
MR GRANT:	*(Unsure)* And stops all that play acting.
PROFESSOR:	They'll have to work their socks off.
MR GRANT:	I might be persuaded. *(To Isla, Jack and Nina)* That doesn't mean you are off the hook. *(To Tank)* Have you found anything? 90
TANK:	*(Sieving)* Just that I like doing this.
JACK:	*(Whispering to Isla)* Mr Grant hasn't noticed.
MR GRANT:	Noticed what?
ISLA:	*(Sadly)* No Kiran.
MR GRANT:	What? 95
ISLA:	Gone.
MR GRANT:	*(Realising)* You're right. Where is he? *(To Jack, Nina and Isla)* Last I saw of Kiran you three were dragging him out of this clearing. What have you done with him? 100
JACK:	Nothing.
MR GRANT:	Is Kiran in the chalet? Tell me he's in the chalet.

ISLA: He's not.

MR GRANT: When I find that boy we are all getting on   105
            a minibus and . . .

ISLA: *(Solemnly)* You won't find him.

MR GRANT: Then where on Earth . . .?

JACK: *(Quietly)* Nowhere.

NINA: Nowhere on Earth.   110

MR GRANT: What are you saying? *(Slowly to Isla) Where*
            has Kiran gone?

ISLA: Back home.

MR GRANT: Home?

ISLA: *(Accepting)* Where he belongs.   115

*Seriously worried, Mr Grant pulls out his mobile
phone and starts to punch in some numbers. Jack
and Nina look up to the sky. Tank and Professor
Anderson glance up, confused.*

*Isla walks away, squeezing the brooch hard, never
wanting to let go.*

Blackout.

Glossary

adamant definite or sure about something

aerial from the air

apochromatic refractor telescope powerful telescope that uses special lenses and refraction to allow astronomers to study space

artefact a crafted object

bemused confused

cease stop

cherish love and take great care of

chronological order order in which events happened

compassion care and sympathy for someone else

conserved kept safe from harm or destruction

contaminated made impure

cosmos universe

desist stop

destiny a person's fate or true calling in life

devastation destruction

dilapidated old, rundown

disintegrating breaking into pieces

distractedly not concentrating

distraught very distressed

emanating spreading out

entity independently existing thing

excavation digging up the ground

fabrication making something up

floundering uncertain, unsure

flummoxed baffled

half-marathon running race of 13.1 miles

hypothesis unproven theory

ice cream headache short period of headache experienced after eating or drinking something very cold

imperative essential

indentation hollowed-out area

in situ in its original place

inordinate abnormally large

intriguing fascinating

light pollution unnecessary artificial light

linear particle accelerator machine in which subatomic particles are speeded up; has many scientific uses including investigating the structure of matter

meteor strike meteor moving through space hitting the Earth

Neolithic a period in history from about 4000 to 2500 BCE

nocturnal taking place at night

petrified terrified and unable to move

predictable expected

prodigal lost (refers to the Parable of the Prodigal Son in the Bible)

reiterated repeated

relic ancient object

sacked ransacked, destroyed

sinister strange, frightening, possibly evil

solar wind stream of charged particles flowing from the sun

sophisticated worldly-wise, cultured and self-assured

spiral galaxy disc-shaped cluster of stars

supernova an exploding star

surreal out of the ordinary, dream-like

tickling a trout gently stroking the belly of a trout so that it becomes quiet and can be caught

Activities

Activity 1: Predictions

In this activity, you will predict what the play could be about.

1   **On your own**, consider the title of the play, *The Finders*. Spend three minutes making a list of all of your ideas about who these 'finders' could be.

2   Then think more deeply about the title and what different events or moments might occur within a play with this title. Write these as bullet points to accompany your list.

3   **In pairs**, swap your list with a partner. Explain to each other the ideas you have written down and see if there are any ideas on your lists that match. Together, choose the most original, imaginative idea from both lists and prepare to share it.

4   Decide on which one of you will act as a spokesperson from your pair to stand up and share your idea with the class.

5   **As a class**, choose a scribe to write down the idea given by each pair until a class list has been made. Keep the list on your classroom wall as you read the play, so that ideas can be ticked, crossed off or added to as you find out more information.

Activity 2: Cast list

In this activity, you will use the cast list to make predictions about the behaviour of the characters in the play.

1   **On your own,** read the cast list very carefully. For each of the characters on the list, write down answers to the following questions:

   a   What does the cast list reveal about this character?
   b   Why might this be important?
   c   Where does this character appear in the cast list and why do you think this is?

2   What predictions can you make about the play, based on the information you are given in the cast list? Fill in a table like the one below:

Information from the cast list	Prediction about the play

3   **In groups of around four,** choose four of the characters from the cast list. Using only the information you are given in the list, improvise a three-minute piece of drama. The characters can meet up anywhere that your group chooses but you must show in their interaction that you have used the information in the cast list.

Activity 3: Tank and Jack

In this activity, you will explore the relationship between Tank and the other students.

1 **On your own**, read Act One, Scene 1 very carefully. Fill in a table like the one below. Write down any quotes where Tank makes fun of somebody or where he is the butt of a joke himself.

Line references	Insults from Tank	Insults about Tank

2 Write down answers to the following questions:

   a What are the differences between Tank and the other students?
   b Why do you think Tank is the first to leave the classroom?

3 **In pairs**, select one person to take the role of Tank and the other to take the role of Jack. Prepare to stage an argument that might happen between the two characters once they have left the classroom. Think carefully about how the argument might begin and the insults that each character might use against the other.

4 Role-play your argument for the class. You should also act as an audience for the performances of other pairs.

5 In the same pairs, consider Tank's character at the end of the play. How has he changed and how have the other characters' perceptions of him changed? Create a short, second role-play between Jack and Tank after Kiran's disappearance. How might they speak and interact differently?

Activity 4: Stage directions

In this activity, you will consider the effect that stage directions have on the performance of a play.

1 **On your own,** read Act One, Scene 3 very carefully, from 'All you need to do is *look*' (line 10) to 'Except school dinners' (line 69).

2 **In groups of around four,** read this part of the scene aloud, each taking the role of one or two characters. Take careful note of the stage directions which tell you how to read your lines.

3 Now substitute the stage directions in column 3 below for those in column 2:

Line refs	Original stage directions	New stage directions
16	*(Whispering to Nina)*	*(Laughing loudly)*
17	*(Guessing)*	*(Offended and tearful)*
24	*(Enthusiastically)*	*(Bored)*
31	*(Isla nods)*	*(Isla shrugs)*
42	*(Impressed)*	*(Annoyed)*
43	*(Quietly to Tank)*	*(Shouting at Tank)*
46	*(Shrugs)*	*(Pleased)*
54	*(Pleased with Kiran)*	*(Dismissively)*
58	*(Jumping back)*	*(Leaning forward excitedly)*
59	*(Smiling)*	*(Not caring)*
64	*(Excited)*	*(Sarcastic)*

4 Re-read the scene with the new stage directions.

5   **In your groups,** discuss the following questions, each **making your own notes** on your answers:

   a   How was the scene different when you performed it the second time?

   b   Which performance made more sense, having already studied some of these characters in earlier scenes?

   c   Would you change, or add, any stage directions for this part of the scene?

6   **On your own,** choose a person that was not in your group to pair up with and share with them what you have found.

Activity 5: Nina's report

In this activity, you will compose Mr Grant's school report for Nina based on what you know about Nina's character.

1 **As a class,** make a list of all of the headings that might be included in a school report. Then decide on what headings should be included in the report you will write for Nina.

2 **In pairs,** make a thought shower of all of the things that you know about Nina. These could include Nina's actions, quotes from her or about her from other characters, and your own opinions about Nina.

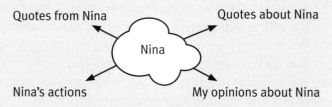

Quotes from Nina   Quotes about Nina

Nina

Nina's actions   My opinions about Nina

3 **On your own,** using the information in your thought shower to help you, write Mr Grant's report for Nina under the headings that you decided on as a class.

Activity 6: Mini sagas

In this activity, you will respond creatively to *The Finders* and are encouraged to consider the most important parts of the play.

1 **On your own,** using your knowledge of the whole play:

   a Write a bullet point list of all of the most important events in the play, in chronological order.

   b Write down the story of *The Finders* in no more than 100 words. You will have to choose the information that you include very carefully so that you keep the most important parts of the plot in your saga.

   c Write down the story of *The Finders* in no more than 50 words. This will mean shortening your saga even further; remember that the story *must make sense* and still include the things that you think are most important in the play.

   d See if you can summarise the play in text message form, using 20 words or less. This will be the most difficult!

2 **In pairs,** share your mini sagas with a partner and ask them to check that none of them are over their word limit. Listen to their sagas and make a note of the different elements that each of you thought needed to be included. Prepare to share the best mini sagas with the class.

Activity 7: Being Kiran

In this activity, you will be asked to empathise more closely with the character of Kiran, the 'outsider in the group', and reflect on his personality traits.

1 **On your own,** look back at Act One of the play. Write down five different words or short phrases to describe Kiran's character during the opening scenes of the play.

2 Imagine you are Kiran during a particularly boring lesson at school. Write down what *he* might jot in the back of his exercise book whilst the teacher is talking.

3 **In pairs:**

   a Discuss with a partner what music Kiran might have on his iPod, giving reasons for your ideas – these should be quotes or direct evidence from the play.

   b Now discuss and list Kiran's 'Top Five' films and books, again giving reasons for each idea. As before, make sure you use quotes or other direct evidence from the play to back up your judgements.

   c Share your ideas with the class.

4 **On your own,** using your knowledge of Kiran across the whole play, create and write his Facebook page. Alternatively, you could write his Twitter feed leading up to the school trip.

Activity 8: A dramatic performance

In this activity, you will need to consider carefully performance aspects of the play, focusing closely on the climactic moments.

1 **In groups**, read Act Three, Scene 3 (from the stage direction '*Jack, Nina and Isla come to their senses*' to the end of the scene). You will need readers for Kiran, Jack, Nina and Isla and one of you should act as director.

2 Talk about how to perform this emotional scene for an audience at a school production of the play. Carefully consider:

   a how to show Kiran's realisation of his true identity
   b how to convey Isla's torment at losing Kiran
   c what moves and actions on stage will bring this scene to life
   d how you might use lights, props and sound effects to add drama to the scene as written.

3 Make a note of each of your group's ideas for the above points of consideration, ready for the feedback session.

4 **As a class**, using your written notes feed back your ideas from the work above, discussing staging issues and how you would overcome any problems or weaknesses.

5 **In groups**, perform this scene as effectively as you can in front of the other groups. You should then act as an audience for their performances.

Activity 9: Pitch perfect!

In this activity, you will need to imagine that the writer/publishers of the play *The Finders* want to adapt it into a blockbuster movie!

1 **In pairs**:

   a Discuss with a partner what makes *The Finders* an exciting, moving piece of drama. Come up with a series of statements.

   b Think carefully and discuss what changes might have to be made to the play for it to work as a film of about an hour and a half.

   c Devise three possible 'tag-lines' (catchy slogans to give a 'feel' for the text) that might be used on posters and/or trailers to 'sell' the film version of *The Finders*.

   d Share your ideas with the class and discuss the process of adapting a play for the cinema screen.

2 **On your own**:

   a You are now ready to see whether anyone would be interested in bringing *The Finders* to the big screen! You are going to write and deliver a 'pitch'; this is a short, persuasive speech aimed at a film producer to convince them that this would be a really great opportunity. The pitch must only last **one minute** when spoken and should aim to excite, enthuse and inspire.

   b Include a brief 'cast list' of possible actors who could effectively play the different roles.

   c After you have practised it, deliver your pitch to the class. You should also act as an audience for others' pitches. The class could vote on which pitch was the most convincing and persuasive.

Activity 10: Icebergs

In this activity, you will reflect on how people do not always say what they think and feel.

1   **In pairs,** choose two characters from the play. Discuss their traits and what things they might keep hidden from others. You could present your evidence from the play in a table like this:

Character	S/he reveals	Evidence	S/he conceals	Evidence

2   Team up with another pair. Share your ideas and discuss your findings.

3   **Work in groups.** You will each need a sheet of A3 plain paper (or larger). On this, draw a large iceberg shape showing the waterline. There should be a small amount of the triangular iceberg above the waterline and a larger proportion beneath.

4   Choose a character each and imagine your characters together in a scene (this could be one from the play itself or an improvisation). Write on the part of the iceberg *above the waterline* each line of dialogue your characters *speak*. Write on the part of the iceberg *below the waterline* what the characters might *really think or feel*. This text should be big enough for an audience to read, as it will not be spoken aloud.

5   Perform your short script to another group, making sure that during the performance your audience can read the characters' unspoken thoughts written on the iceberg. Then discuss why certain characters might conceal their true thoughts and feelings.

Activity 11: A sombre school assembly

In this activity, you will imagine what words might be spoken during an assembly after Kiran's disappearance. It is likely that the school will eventually treat it as 'unexplained' and may presume kidnapping, runaway or even death . . .

1 **In groups:**

   a Discuss what Mr Grant, the Professor and Tank might believe or not believe about Kiran's disappearance.

   b Discuss what Isla, Nina and Jack might reveal or conceal about what really happened to Kiran and why they might do this. Explore what emotions each might experience about withholding the truth.

2 **In pairs:**

   a Choose one character, or make up a new character (e.g. the Headteacher, another classmate), who might speak at a tribute assembly to Kiran.

   b Script this character's tribute speech, basing their words on what you know about Kiran and how his disappearance may have been perceived by the character you have chosen or created.

3 Perform your tribute speech for another group. You should also act as an audience for their speech.

Activity 12: A sequel to *The Finders*!

In this activity, you will come up with creative ideas for a sequel to the play *The Finders*, set ten years after the events in the original.

1   **In pairs**:

   a   Choose three characters other than Kiran from the play. Imagine ten years have passed since Kiran returned 'home'. Discuss what each character might be doing and how they might have come to terms with what happened.

   b   Write a short dialogue between two of your three characters, as they meet up ten years after the events in *The Finders*. What might they talk about? How will they approach the subject of Kiran? How has it affected their own lives and outlook on the world?

2   Perform your short role-play to the class, taking feedback as appropriate.

3   **On your own**:

   a   You are now going to come up with some ideas for *The Finders 2*, which should be set ten years after the events of the original. Your 'sequel' should incorporate characters from the original along with any new characters you would like to create.

   b   You need to present your ideas in the form of a cast list, plot summary and short sample scene.